THIS BOOK BELONGS TO

_____

START DATE

_____

SHE READS TRUTH

FOUNDERS

FOUNDER
Raechel Myers

CO-FOUNDER
Amanda Bible Williams

EXECUTIVE

CHIEF EXECUTIVE OFFICER
Ryan Myers

EDITORIAL

MANAGING EDITOR
Lindsey Jacobi, MDiv

PRODUCTION EDITOR
Hannah Little, MTS

ASSOCIATE EDITOR
Kayla De La Torre, MAT

COPY EDITOR
Becca Owens, MA

CREATIVE

SENIOR ART DIRECTOR
Annie Glover

DESIGN MANAGER
Kelsea Allen

DESIGNERS
Savannah Ault
Ashley Phillips

MARKETING

MARKETING LEAD
Kelsey Chapman

PRODUCT MARKETING MANAGER
Krista Squibb

CONTENT MARKETING STRATEGIST
Tameshia Williams, ThM

SOCIAL MEDIA SPECIALIST
Bella Ponce

OPERATIONS

OPERATIONS DIRECTOR
Allison Sutton

COMMUNITY ENGAGEMENT

COMMUNITY ENGAGEMENT MANAGER
Delaney Coleman

COMMUNITY ENGAGEMENT SPECIALISTS
Cait Baggerman
Katy McKnight

SHIPPING

SHIPPING MANAGER
Marian Welch

FULFILLMENT LEAD
Hannah Song

FULFILLMENT SPECIALISTS
Bonnie Nickander
Kelsey Simpson

SUBSCRIPTION INQUIRIES
orders@shereadstruth.com

CONTRIBUTORS

PHOTOGRAPHY
Alyssa Bustin (50)
Kelsey Butcher (84)
Alyssa Hollis (143)
Hannah-Grace Jost (112)
Rachel Loewen (41, 69, 109, 185)

RECIPES
Taylor Lamb (75)
Paul and Cami Little (160)

SPECIAL THANKS
Jessica Lamb, MA
Beth Joseph
Kara Gause
Bailey Gillespie
Jeremy Mitchell
Abbey Benson
Davis Camp DeLisi
Lauren Haag

SHE READS TRUTH™

© 2021, 2025 by She Reads Truth, LLC
All rights reserved. First edition 2021.
Second edition 2025.

All photography used by permission.

ISBN 978-1-962221-46-7

1 2 3 4 5 6 7 8 9 10

Though the dates, locations, and individuals in this book have been carefully researched, scholars disagree on many of these topics.

Research support provided by Logos Bible Software™. Learn more at logos.com.

@SHEREADSTRUTH

Download the She Reads Truth app, available for iOS and Android

Subscribe to the She Reads Truth Podcast

This book was printed offset in Nashville, Tennessee, on 70# Lynx Opaque. Cover is 100# Cougar Opaque with a soft touch lamination.

ACTS

The birth of the early Church is the story of God's kingdom alive in His people.

Amanda

Amanda Bible Williams
CO-FOUNDER

Remember the time Peter walked on water? It was an early morning on the Sea of Galilee, the day after Jesus miraculously fed the five thousand. The disciples saw Jesus walking toward their boat, holy feet standing steady on the waves. Peter, in his trademark zeal, asked to be empowered to do the same. "Lord, if it's you,...command me to come to you on the water" (Mt 14:28). Jesus offered a one-word reply: "Come." So Peter did. He walked on water toward Jesus...until moments later when the sight of the wind and waves replaced his confidence with fear and he began to sink.

It's an illustration so vivid that Peter's hard-won lesson is impossible to miss. Like Peter, our central call is to stay focused on Jesus as He empowers us, through the gift of His Spirit, to do what we've been called to do.

This same Peter is a key figure in the book of Acts. Despite opposition and imprisonment, he consistently kept his eyes focused on Jesus as he helped build and lead the early Church. The book of Acts is the history book of the earliest Christians, like Peter, who were a brand-new community of Jesus-followers learning how to live out the gospel that had newly transformed every aspect of their lives and worldview. The inspiring, action-packed narrative recounts the spread of Jesus's message and the growth of the early Church. But it's important to remember that these first church planters and preachers were not superheroes; they were sinners saved by grace, ordinary people with an extraordinary Savior. The spread of the Church was fueled not by flawless strategy but by earnest faith in Jesus.

Pastor and theologian N. T. Wright notes that the book of Acts shows us how "the method of the kingdom will match the message of the kingdom." The gospel is the good news of Jesus for the sinner, the suffering, the vulnerable, the misunderstood, and the overconfident. And the gospel is spread by these same unlikely ambassadors—not by their might or power, but by the Holy Spirit living in and among them.

In this six-week study, we'll read the book of Acts in its entirety and discover God's plan for His Church. We'll explore the book's themes through guided note-taking and weekly reflection questions, and we'll learn about key people and places in this history book of the early Church. Don't miss the "God the Spirit" extra on page 120, which provides important context for the work of the Spirit that you'll see throughout Acts.

The birth of the early Church is the story of God's kingdom alive in His people and spread by His Spirit at work in us. It is the true story of where we came from and where we are going. As you set out to read, ask God to guide you by His Spirit even now, training your eyes to focus on Him in carrying out the work He's called us to do.

FREIGHT DISPLAY

DEFGHIJKLM
QRSTUVWXYZ

ITALIC

abcdefghijklm
nopqrstuvwxyz

SEMIBOLD

abcdefghijklm
nopqrstuvwxyz

FREIGHT SANS

DEFGHIJKLMN
RSTUVWXYZ

DESIGN ON PURPOSE

At She Reads Truth, we believe in pairing the inherently beautiful Word of God with the aesthetic beauty it deserves. Each of our resources is thoughtfully and artfully designed to highlight the beauty, goodness, and truth of Scripture in a way that reflects the themes of each curated reading plan.

For this Reading Guide, we incorporated the entire Freight font family, hinting at the growth and diversity of the early Church. The reading plan also features hand lettering to add warmth and familiarity. The photography is centered around modern daily life—travel, gatherings, and meeting spaces—to help connect this first-century account with today's context.

Scrapbook and travel journal designs inspired much of our layout, a nod to the preservation of the Church's history in Acts as well as the journey of the gospel from Jerusalem to Rome. The book's warm palette reminds us of the camaraderie and selflessness of the early Church, and red, the primary color, represents the Holy Spirit's vibrant presence dwelling in God's people.

HOW TO USE THIS BOOK

She Reads Truth is a community of women dedicated to reading the Word of God every day. In this **Acts** reading plan, we will read the book of Acts, along with complementary passages of Scripture, to see how Jesus's call to take the gospel into the world was carried out by believers through the power of the Holy Spirit.

READ & REFLECT

Your **Acts** book focuses primarily on Scripture, with added features to come alongside your time with God's Word.

SCRIPTURE READING

Designed for a Monday start, this book presents the book of Acts in daily readings, along with additional passages curated to show how the theme of the main reading can be found throughout Scripture.

🔖 *Additional passages are marked in your daily reading with the Going Deeper heading.*

REFLECTION QUESTIONS

Each week features questions and space for personal reflection.

COMMUNITY & CONVERSATION

You can start reading this book at any time! If you want to join women from Sulphur Springs to Slovakia as they read along with you, join us in the **Acts** reading plan through our app or website and podcast.

SHE READS TRUTH APP

Devotionals corresponding to each daily reading can be found in the **Acts** reading plan in the She Reads Truth app. You can use the app to participate in community discussion and more.

GRACE DAY

Use Saturdays to catch up on your reading, pray, and rest in the presence of the Lord.

WEEKLY TRUTH

Sundays are set aside for Scripture memorization.

See tips for memorizing Scripture on page 196.

EXTRAS

This book features additional tools to help you gain a deeper understanding of the text, including a bookmark to help you take notes on the key themes as you read. See page 20 for more on how to use your bookmark!

Find a complete list of extras on page 13.

SHEREADSTRUTH.COM

The **Acts** reading plan and devotionals will also be available at SheReadsTruth.com as the community reads each day. Invite your family, friends, and neighbors to read along with you!

SHE READS TRUTH PODCAST

Subscribe to the She Reads Truth Podcast, and join our founders and their guests each week as they talk about what you'll read in the week ahead.

*Tune into episodes 311–316 for our **Acts** series.*

Table of Contents

ACTS 12:24

But the word of God spread and multiplied.

WEEK 3

WEEK 4

ACTS 17:28

For in him we live and
move and have our being.

Extras

Recipes

KEY VERSE

"BUT YOU WILL RECEIVE POWER WHEN THE HOLY SPIRIT HAS

COME ON YOU, AND YOU WILL BE MY WITNESSES IN JERUSALEM,

IN ALL JUDEA AND SAMARIA, AND TO THE ENDS OF THE EARTH."

Acts 1:8

SHE READS

Acts

TIME TO READ ACTS

2 Hours, 15 Minutes

ON THE TIMELINE

The book of Acts is traditionally credited to a physician named Luke, the author of the Gospel of Luke and a traveling companion of Paul. Both Luke and Acts are believed to have been written at the same time—during the early-to-mid AD 60s after the conclusion of the events covered in Acts. The events recorded in Acts took place after the resurrection of Christ in AD 33 and concluded around AD 62 or 63.

A LITTLE BACKGROUND

Acts provides biographical glimpses of some of the early apostles as they spread the good news of Jesus first in Jerusalem and then to the world around the Mediterranean. Peter, Philip, and a few others were heavily involved in the Church's spread to the Jewish people in Jerusalem, Judea, and Samaria, while Paul primarily focused on ministry to the Gentiles.

Paul's typical missionary strategy was to go to a familiar place in each city he visited—usually a synagogue—and proclaim the gospel first to local Jewish people. The speed with which he shifted his focus to Gentiles outside the synagogue depended on how he was received within the synagogue. Before leaving a town, Paul united Jewish and Gentile converts to form a local church.

MESSAGE & PURPOSE

GIVE THANKS FOR THE BOOK OF ACTS

The book of Acts emphasizes the work of God through the Holy Spirit in the lives of people who devoted themselves to Jesus Christ, especially Paul as he led the Gentile missionary endeavor. The Christian church was built—person by person in city after city—through the dynamic power of the Holy Spirit working through followers of Jesus.

The book of Acts bridges the years between those who walked with Jesus firsthand and those who came to faith through their testimony. Jesus's story did not end with His ascension to heaven forty days after His resurrection; it continues through the lives of His followers. Acts shows us how Jesus's call to take the gospel into the world was carried out by the apostles and other believers by the power of the Holy Spirit. It also gives us the context for much of the New Testament, especially the letters Paul wrote to the churches he helped establish during his missionary journeys.

Groups and Places in Acts

The gospel of Jesus Christ unifies people separated by culture, race, gender, vocation, and social standing. For those living in the Roman Empire in the first century, this unity was unusual and astonishing. Acts repeatedly calls attention to this theme by identifying people not just by name but by the groups that otherwise separated them, demonstrating the unifying nature of the gospel.

There are seven key groups in the book of Acts:

THE APOSTLES

Apostle means "one who is sent." In the New Testament, this term most often refers to the twelve disciples (with Matthias taking the place of Judas after his death) who walked with Jesus, though it is also used for other early Church leaders.

JEWS / HEBREWS / ISRAELITES

These names are all used for the descendants of Abraham with whom God made a covenant and who were devoted to God and His law given to Moses at Mount Sinai.

SAMARITANS

This group consisted of descendants of Israelites from the northern kingdom of Israel who intermarried with Gentiles after the Assyrian Empire repopulated the region. They had little contact with the Jewish people because of ethnic and religious differences.

GENTILES

The word literally means "the nations," signifying everyone who was not Jewish. They were regarded by most Jewish people as unclean.

GOD-FEARERS

Gentiles who worshiped Israel's God but had not fully converted to the Jewish faith were called God-fearers. They did not necessarily adhere to the Old Testament laws about food restrictions or circumcision.

ROMANS

People called Romans were official citizens, by birth or legal decree, who were protected by Roman law and granted additional legal rights in the Roman Empire.

GREEKS

This was the group of people born in Greece or Greek-speaking people living in the eastern part of the Roman Empire.

PLACES IN ACTS

In the Great Commission, Jesus told His followers they would be His witnesses "in Jerusalem, in all Judea and Samaria, and to the ends of the earth" (Ac 1:8). In the first century, many considered the Roman Empire to reach the ends of the earth. In this sense, the progression Jesus described is precisely what happens in the book of Acts as the gospel spread from Jerusalem, Judea, and Samaria, to the ends of the Roman Empire.

1 JERUSALEM

Located in nearly the same location as the city established during King David's reign, Jerusalem was Israel's capital city and the heart of Jewish history and culture.

2 JUDEA

Also known as Judah and located south of Samaria, the region of Judea ranged from the eastern border of the Jordan River and Dead Sea to its western border along the Mediterranean Sea.

3 SAMARIA

Located in modern-day Syria and Lebanon, Samaria reached from the Jordan River west to the Mediterranean Sea.

4 ASIA MINOR

Located in modern-day Turkey, Asia Minor included the regions of Galatia and Cappadocia and the cities of Derbe, Lystra, Ephesus, Colossae, Miletus, and Antioch.

5 MACEDONIA AND ACHAIA

Located in modern-day Romania, Serbia, Bulgaria, Macedonia, and Greece, the regions of Macedonia and Achaia included the cities of Thessalonica, Philippi, Berea, Athens, and Corinth.

6 ROME, SICILY, AND MALTA

Rome was the capital city of the vast Roman Empire. Sicily and Malta are two islands off the coast of Italy.

Key Themes in Acts

▼

The work and role of the Holy Spirit, the development of the early Church, and the spread of the gospel are all key themes in Acts. Use the space on the next page to create your own key for marking each theme in your daily Acts reading. For example, you might highlight each theme in a certain color or place a unique symbol in the margin next to each occurrence. Taking notes will help you answer the repeated reflection questions provided at the end of each week.

CREATE YOUR KEY

Find the bookmark inserted into your Reading Guide to copy your key and create a quick reference guide to use as you read!

◆ 1

THE HOLY SPIRIT

Mark any time the Holy Spirit is mentioned, a miracle occurs, or where the text points to the fulfillment of Jesus's promise to equip the Church with the Holy Spirit.

◆ 2

THE EARLY CHURCH

Take note of how members of the early Church cared for one another, handled conflict, endured persecution, and relied on God's provision.

◆ 3

THE SPREAD OF THE GOSPEL

Look for times where the gospel is carried to different groups throughout Judea, Samaria, and the rest of the world. Mark where the text points to God's desire for all people to come to salvation in Him.

"But you will receive power when the Holy Spirit has come on you, and you will be my witnesses in Jerusalem, in all Judea and Samaria, and to the ends of the earth."

ACTS 1:8

Acts 1; Matthew 28:16–20; John 16:7–14

The Ascension

ACTS 1

PROLOGUE

[1] I wrote the first narrative, Theophilus, about all that Jesus began to do and teach [2] until the day he was taken up, after he had given instructions through the Holy Spirit to the apostles he had chosen. [3] After he had suffered, he also presented himself alive to them by many convincing proofs, appearing to them over a period of forty days and speaking about the kingdom of God.

THE HOLY SPIRIT PROMISED

[4] While he was with them, he commanded them not to leave Jerusalem, but to wait for the Father's promise. "Which," he said, "you have heard me speak about; [5] for John baptized with water, but you will be baptized with the Holy Spirit in a few days."

[6] So when they had come together, they asked him, "Lord, are you restoring the kingdom to Israel at this time?"

[7] He said to them, "It is not for you to know times or periods that the Father has set by his own authority. [8] But you will receive power when the Holy Spirit has come on you, and you will be my witnesses in Jerusalem, in all Judea and Samaria, and to the ends of the earth."

> **JERUSALEM
> AD 33**
>
> *The "You Are Here" icon will help you follow the location and approximate date of each main event from the daily reading in Acts.*

⁹ After he had said this, he was taken up as they were watching, and a cloud took him out of their sight. ¹⁰ While he was going, they were gazing into heaven, and suddenly two men in white clothes stood by them. ¹¹ They said, "Men of Galilee, why do you stand looking up into heaven? This same Jesus, who has been taken from you into heaven, will come in the same way that you have seen him going into heaven."

UNITED IN PRAYER

¹² Then they returned to Jerusalem from the Mount of Olives, which is near Jerusalem—a Sabbath day's journey away. ¹³ When they arrived, they went to the room upstairs where they were staying: Peter, John, James, Andrew, Philip, Thomas, Bartholomew, Matthew, James the son of Alphaeus, Simon the Zealot, and Judas the son of James. ¹⁴ They all were continually united in prayer, along with the women, including Mary the mother of Jesus, and his brothers.

MATTHIAS CHOSEN

¹⁵ In those days Peter stood up among the brothers and sisters—the number of people who were together was about a hundred twenty—and said, ¹⁶ "Brothers and sisters, it was necessary that the Scripture be fulfilled that the Holy Spirit through the mouth of David foretold about Judas, who became a guide to those who arrested Jesus. ¹⁷ For he was one of our number and shared in this ministry." ¹⁸ Now this man acquired a field with his unrighteous wages. He fell headfirst, his body burst open and his intestines spilled out. ¹⁹ This became known to all the residents of Jerusalem, so that in their own language that field is called *Hakeldama* (that is, "Field of Blood"). ²⁰ "For it is written in the Book of Psalms:

Let his dwelling become desolate;
let no one live in it; and
Let someone else take his position.

²¹ "Therefore, from among the men who have accompanied us during the whole time the Lord Jesus went in and out among us— ²² beginning from the baptism of John until the day he was taken up from us—from among these, it is necessary that one become a witness with us of his resurrection."

²³ So they proposed two: Joseph, called Barsabbas, who was also known as Justus, and Matthias. ²⁴ Then they prayed, "You, Lord, know everyone's hearts; show which of these two you have chosen ²⁵ to take the place in this apostolic ministry that Judas left to go where he belongs." ²⁶ Then they cast lots for them, and the lot fell to Matthias and he was added to the eleven apostles.

🔖 GOING DEEPER

MATTHEW 28:16-20

THE GREAT COMMISSION

¹⁶ The eleven disciples traveled to Galilee, to the mountain where Jesus had directed them. ¹⁷ When they saw him, they worshiped, but some doubted. ¹⁸ Jesus came near and said to them, "All authority has been given to me in heaven and on earth. ¹⁹ Go, therefore, and make disciples of all nations, baptizing them in the name of the Father and of the Son and of the Holy Spirit, ²⁰ teaching them to observe everything I have commanded you. And remember, I am with you always, to the end of the age."

JOHN 16:7-14

⁷ "Nevertheless, I am telling you the truth. It is for your benefit that I go away, because if I don't go away the Counselor will not come to you. If I go, I will send him to you. ⁸ When he comes, he will convict the world about sin, righteousness, and judgment: ⁹ About sin, because they do not believe in me; ¹⁰ about righteousness, because I am going to the Father and you will no longer see me; ¹¹ and about judgment, because the ruler of this world has been judged.

¹² "I still have many things to tell you, but you can't bear them now. ¹³ When the Spirit of truth comes, he will guide you into all the truth. For he will not speak on his own, but he will speak whatever he hears. He will also declare to you what is to come. ¹⁴ He will glorify me, because he will take from what is mine and declare it to you."

Notes

DATE

Acts 2; Joel 2:28–32; John 7:37–39

The Day of Pentecost

▶ JERUSALEM
AD 33

ACTS 2

PENTECOST

¹ When the day of Pentecost had arrived, they were all together in one place. ² Suddenly a sound like that of a violent rushing wind came from heaven, and it filled the whole house where they were staying. ³ They saw tongues like flames of fire that separated and rested on each one of them. ⁴ Then they were all filled with the Holy Spirit and began to speak in different tongues, as the Spirit enabled them.

⁵ Now there were Jews staying in Jerusalem, devout people from every nation under heaven. ⁶ When this sound occurred, a crowd came together and was confused because each one heard them speaking in his own language. ⁷ They were astounded and amazed, saying, "Look, aren't all these who are speaking Galileans? ⁸ How is it that each of us can hear them in our own native language? ⁹ Parthians, Medes, Elamites; those who live in Mesopotamia, in Judea and Cappadocia, Pontus and Asia, ¹⁰ Phrygia and Pamphylia, Egypt and the parts of Libya near Cyrene; visitors from Rome (both Jews and converts), ¹¹ Cretans and Arabs—we hear them declaring the magnificent acts of God in our own tongues." ¹² They were all astounded and perplexed, saying to one another, "What does this mean?" ¹³ But some sneered and said, "They're drunk on new wine."

PETER'S SERMON

¹⁴ Peter stood up with the Eleven, raised his voice, and proclaimed to them, "Fellow Jews and all you residents of Jerusalem, let this be known to you, and pay

attention to my words. ¹⁵ For these people are not drunk, as you suppose, since it's only nine in the morning. ¹⁶ On the contrary, this is what was spoken through the prophet Joel:

¹⁷ And it will be in the last days, says God,
that I will pour out my Spirit on all people;
then your sons and your daughters will prophesy,
your young men will see visions,
and your old men will dream dreams.
¹⁸ I will even pour out my Spirit
on my servants in those days, both men and women
and they will prophesy.
¹⁹ I will display wonders in the heaven above
and signs on the earth below:
blood and fire and a cloud of smoke.
²⁰ The sun will be turned to darkness
and the moon to blood
before the great and glorious day of the Lord comes.

²¹ Then everyone who calls on the name of the Lord will be saved.

²² "Fellow Israelites, listen to these words: This Jesus of Nazareth was a man attested to you by God with miracles, wonders, and signs that God did among you through him, just as you yourselves know. ²³ Though he was delivered up according to God's determined plan and foreknowledge, you used lawless people to nail him to a cross and kill him. ²⁴ God raised him up, ending the pains of death, because it was not possible for him to be held by death. ²⁵ For David says of him:

I saw the Lord ever before me;
because he is at my right hand,
I will not be shaken.
²⁶ Therefore my heart is glad
and my tongue rejoices.
Moreover, my flesh will rest in hope,
²⁷ because you will not abandon me in Hades
or allow your holy one to see decay.
²⁸ You have revealed the paths of life to me;
you will fill me with gladness
in your presence.

²⁹ "Brothers and sisters, I can confidently speak to you about the patriarch David: He is both dead and buried, and his tomb is with us to this day. ³⁰ Since he was a prophet, he knew that God had sworn an oath to him to seat one of his descendants on his throne. ³¹ Seeing what was to come, he spoke concerning the resurrection of the Messiah: He was not abandoned in Hades, and his flesh did not experience decay.

³² "God has raised this Jesus; we are all witnesses of this. ³³ Therefore, since he has been exalted to the right hand of God and has received from the Father the promised Holy Spirit, he has poured out what you both see and hear. ³⁴ For it was not David who ascended into the heavens, but he himself says:

The Lord declared to my Lord,
'Sit at my right hand
³⁵ until I make your enemies your footstool.'

³⁶ "Therefore let all the house of Israel know with certainty that God has made this Jesus, whom you crucified, both Lord and Messiah."

CALL TO REPENTANCE

³⁷ When they heard this, they were pierced to the heart and said to Peter and the rest of the apostles, "Brothers, what should we do?"

³⁸ Peter replied, "Repent and be baptized, each of you, in the name of Jesus Christ for the forgiveness of your sins, and you will receive the gift of the Holy Spirit. ³⁹ For the promise is for you and for your children, and for all who are far off, as many as the Lord our God will call." ⁴⁰ With many other words he testified and strongly urged them, saying, "Be saved from this corrupt generation!" ⁴¹ So those who accepted his message were baptized, and that day about three thousand people were added to them.

A GENEROUS AND GROWING CHURCH

⁴² They devoted themselves to the apostles' teaching, to the fellowship, to the breaking of bread, and to prayer.

[43] Everyone was filled with awe, and many wonders and signs were being performed through the apostles. [44] Now all the believers were together and held all things in common. [45] They sold their possessions and property and distributed the proceeds to all, as any had need. [46] Every day they devoted themselves to meeting together in the temple, and broke bread from house to house. They ate their food with joyful and sincere hearts, [47] praising God and enjoying the favor of all the people. Every day the Lord added to their number those who were being saved.

◖ GOING DEEPER

JOEL 2:28–32
GOD'S PROMISE OF HIS SPIRIT

[28] After this
I will pour out my Spirit on all humanity;
then your sons and your daughters will prophesy,
your old men will have dreams,
and your young men will see visions.
[29] I will even pour out my Spirit
on the male and female slaves in those days.
[30] I will display wonders
in the heavens and on the earth:
blood, fire, and columns of smoke.
[31] The sun will be turned to darkness
and the moon to blood
before the great and terrible day of the LORD comes.
[32] Then everyone who calls
on the name of the LORD will be saved,
for there will be an escape
for those on Mount Zion and in Jerusalem,
as the LORD promised,
among the survivors the LORD calls.

JOHN 7:37–39
THE PROMISE OF THE SPIRIT

[37] On the last and most important day of the festival, Jesus stood up and cried out, "If anyone is thirsty, let him come to me and drink. [38] The one who believes in me, as the Scripture has said, will have streams of living water flow from deep within him." [39] He said this about the Spirit. Those who believed in Jesus were going to receive the Spirit, for the Spirit had not yet been given because Jesus had not yet been glorified.

Notes

DATE

◆ SEQUENCE LISTED IN ACTS 2:9–11

13 ROME

Adriatic Sea

8 ASIA

Tyrrhenian Sea

14 CRETE

Mediterranean Sea

12 CYRENE

MAP

The Places of Pentecost

During the biblical period, Jewish adult males were required to celebrate the Festival of Pentecost. Also known as the Feast of Weeks or the Feast of Harvest, this festival commemorated the giving of the law at Mount Sinai (Ex 23:16; 34:22) by offering the firstfruits of the spring harvest. Acts 2 records how, during Pentecost, the Holy Spirit fell upon the disciples gathered in the upper room and gave them the supernatural ability to speak in foreign languages. Crowds that had journeyed "from every nation under heaven" (Ac 2:5) to Jerusalem for the festival heard their own language being spoken and were amazed.

The list of places named in Acts 2 is more than just a roster of attendance. The acknowledgement of these nations by the Holy Spirit shows how God included the dispersed nations of the world in His kingdom with the birth of the Church.

Caspian Sea

Black Sea

7 PONTUS

6 CAPPADOCIA

9 PHRYGIA

1 PARTHIAN EMPIRE

2 MEDIA

4 MESOPOTAMIA

10 PAMPHYLIA

Tigris River

3 ELAM

JERUSALEM

5 JUDEA

Euphrates River

11 EGYPT

15 ARABIA

Nile River

Red Sea

0 MI   100   200

N

0 KM   100   200   300   400

REPENT AND TURN BACK, SO THAT YOUR SINS MAY BE

WIPED OUT, THAT SEASONS OF REFRESHING MAY COME

FROM THE PRESENCE OF THE LORD.

Acts 3:19–20

Acts 3; Deuteronomy 18:17–19; Mark 1:14–15

Preaching in Solomon's Colonnade

ACTS 3

HEALING OF A LAME MAN

JERUSALEM
AD 33

[1] Now Peter and John were going up to the temple for the time of prayer at three in the afternoon. [2] A man who was lame from birth was being carried there. He was placed each day at the temple gate called Beautiful, so that he could beg from those entering the temple. [3] When he saw Peter and John about to enter the temple, he asked for money. [4] Peter, along with John, looked straight at him and said, "Look at us." [5] So he turned to them, expecting to get something from them. [6] But Peter said, "I don't have silver or gold, but what I do have, I give you: In the name of Jesus Christ of Nazareth, get up and walk!" [7] Then, taking him by the right hand he raised him up, and at once his feet and ankles became strong. [8] So he jumped up and started to walk, and he entered the temple with them—walking, leaping, and praising God. [9] All the people saw him walking and praising God, [10] and they recognized that he was the one who used to sit and beg at the Beautiful Gate of the temple. So they were filled with awe and astonishment at what had happened to him.

[11] While he was holding on to Peter and John, all the people, utterly astonished, ran toward them in what is called Solomon's Colonnade. [12] When Peter saw this, he addressed the people: "Fellow Israelites, why are you amazed at this? Why do you stare at us, as though we had made him walk by our own power or godliness?

[13] The God of Abraham, Isaac, and Jacob, the God of our ancestors, has glorified his servant Jesus,

whom you handed over and denied before Pilate, though he had decided to release him. [14] You denied the Holy and Righteous One and asked to have a murderer released to you. [15] You killed the source of life, whom God raised from the dead; we are witnesses of this. [16] By faith in his name, his name has made this man strong, whom you see and know. So the faith that comes through Jesus has given him this perfect health in front of all of you.

[17] "And now, brothers and sisters, I know that you acted in ignorance, just as your leaders also did. [18] In this way God fulfilled what he had predicted through all the prophets—that his Messiah would suffer. [19] Therefore repent and turn back, so that your sins may be wiped out, [20] that seasons of refreshing may come from the presence of the Lord, and that he may send Jesus, who has been appointed for you as the Messiah. [21] Heaven must receive him until the time of the restoration of all things, which God spoke about through his holy prophets from the beginning. [22] Moses said: The Lord your God will raise up for you a prophet like me from among your brothers. You must listen to everything he tells you. [23] And everyone who does not listen to that prophet will be completely cut off from the people.

[24] "In addition, all the prophets who have spoken, from Samuel and those after him, have also foretold these days. [25] You are the sons of the prophets and of the covenant that God made with your ancestors, saying to Abraham, And all the families of the earth will be blessed through your offspring. [26] God raised up his servant and sent him first to you to bless you by turning each of you from your evil ways."

❦ GOING DEEPER

DEUTERONOMY 18:17–19

[17] Then the LORD said to me, "They have spoken well. [18] I will raise up for them a prophet like you from among their brothers. I will put my words in his mouth, and he will tell them everything I command him. [19] I will hold accountable whoever does not listen to my words that he speaks in my name."

MARK 1:14–15

[14] After John was arrested, Jesus went to Galilee, proclaiming the good news of God: [15] "The time is fulfilled, and the kingdom of God has come near. Repent and believe the good news!"

Notes

DATE

No Other Name

DAY 4

Acts 4:1–22; Isaiah 45:5–7; 1 John 5:12

ACTS 4:1–22

PETER AND JOHN ARRESTED

¹ While they were speaking to the people, the priests, the captain of the temple police, and the Sadducees confronted them, ² because they were annoyed that they were teaching the people and proclaiming in Jesus the resurrection of the dead. ³ So they seized them and took them into custody until the next day since it was already evening. ⁴ But many of those who heard the message believed, and the number of the men came to about five thousand.

PETER AND JOHN FACE THE JEWISH LEADERSHIP

⁵ The next day, their rulers, elders, and scribes assembled in Jerusalem ⁶ with Annas the high priest, Caiaphas, John, Alexander, and all the members of the high-priestly family. ⁷ After they had Peter and John stand before them, they began to question them: "By what power or in what name have you done this?"

⁸ Then Peter was filled with the Holy Spirit and said to them, "Rulers of the people and elders: ⁹ If we are being examined today about a good deed done to a disabled man, by what means he was healed, ¹⁰ let it be known to all of you and to all the people of Israel, that by the name of Jesus Christ of Nazareth, whom you crucified and whom God raised from the dead—by him this man is standing here before you healthy. ¹¹ This Jesus is

the stone rejected by you builders,
which has become the cornerstone.

¹² There is salvation in no one else, for there is no other name under heaven given to people by which we must be saved."

THE BOLDNESS OF THE DISCIPLES

¹³ When they observed the boldness of Peter and John and realized that they were uneducated and untrained men, they were amazed and recognized that they had been with Jesus. ¹⁴ And since they saw the man who had been healed standing with them, they had nothing to say in opposition. ¹⁵ After they ordered them to leave the Sanhedrin, they conferred among themselves, ¹⁶ saying, "What should we do with these men? For an obvious sign has been done through them, clear to everyone living in Jerusalem, and we cannot deny it. ¹⁷ But so that this does not spread any further among the people, let's threaten them against speaking to anyone in this name again." ¹⁸ So they called for them and ordered them not to speak or teach at all in the name of Jesus.

¹⁹ Peter and John answered them, "Whether it's right in the sight of God for us to listen to you rather than to God, you decide; ²⁰ for we are unable to stop speaking about what we have seen and heard."

[21] After threatening them further, they released them. They found no way to punish them because the people were all giving glory to God over what had been done. [22] For this sign of healing had been performed on a man over forty years old.

♥ GOING DEEPER

ISAIAH 45:5–7

[5] I am the LORD, and there is no other;
there is no God but me.
I will strengthen you,
though you do not know me,
[6] so that all may know from the rising of the sun to its setting
that there is no one but me.
I am the LORD, and there is no other.
[7] I form light and create darkness,
I make success and create disaster;
I am the LORD, who does all these things.

1 JOHN 5:12

The one who has the Son has life. The one who does not have the Son of God does not have life.

Notes

DATE

Acts 4:23–37; 5:1–11; Deuteronomy 15:4–6; John 17:20–23

All Things
in Common

▶ **JERUSALEM
AD 33**

ACTS 4:23–37

PRAYER FOR BOLDNESS

²³ After they were released, they went to their own people and reported everything the chief priests and the elders had said to them. ²⁴ When they heard this, they raised their voices together to God and said, "Master, you are the one who made the heaven, the earth, and the sea, and everything in them. ²⁵ You said through the Holy Spirit, by the mouth of our father David your servant:

> Why do the Gentiles rage
> and the peoples plot futile things?
> ²⁶ The kings of the earth take their stand
> and the rulers assemble together
> against the Lord and against his Messiah.

²⁷ "For, in fact, in this city both Herod and Pontius Pilate, with the Gentiles and the people of Israel, assembled together against your holy servant Jesus, whom you anointed, ²⁸ to do whatever your hand and your will had predestined to take place. ²⁹ And now, Lord, consider their threats, and grant that your servants may speak your word with all boldness, ³⁰ while you stretch out your hand for healing, and signs and wonders are performed through the name of your holy servant Jesus." ³¹ When they had prayed, the place where they were assembled was shaken, and they were all filled with the Holy Spirit and began to speak the word of God boldly.

Notes

³² Now the entire group of those who believed were of one heart and mind, and no one claimed that any of his possessions was his own, but instead they held everything in common. ³³ With great power the apostles were giving testimony to the resurrection of the Lord Jesus, and great grace was on all of them.

³⁴ For there was not a needy person among them because all those who owned lands or houses sold them, brought the proceeds of what was sold, ³⁵ and laid them at the apostles' feet.

This was then distributed to each person as any had need.

³⁶ Joseph, a Levite from Cyprus by birth, the one the apostles called Barnabas (which is translated Son of Encouragement), ³⁷ sold a field he owned, brought the money, and laid it at the apostles' feet.

ACTS 5:1–11

LYING TO THE HOLY SPIRIT

¹ But a man named Ananias, with his wife Sapphira, sold a piece of property. ² However, he kept back part of the proceeds with his wife's knowledge, and brought a portion of it and laid it at the apostles' feet.

³ "Ananias," Peter asked, "why has Satan filled your heart to lie to the Holy Spirit and keep back part of the proceeds of the land? ⁴ Wasn't it yours while you possessed it? And after it was sold, wasn't it at your disposal? Why is it that you planned this thing in your heart? You have not lied to people but to God." ⁵ When he heard these words, Ananias dropped dead, and a great fear came on all who heard. ⁶ The young men got up, wrapped his body, carried him out, and buried him.

⁷ About three hours later, his wife came in, not knowing what had happened. ⁸ "Tell me," Peter asked her, "did you sell the land for this price?"

"Yes," she said, "for that price."

⁹ Then Peter said to her, "Why did you agree to test the Spirit of the Lord? Look, the feet of those who have buried your husband are at the door, and they will carry you out."

¹⁰ Instantly she dropped dead at his feet. When the young men came in, they found her dead, carried her out, and buried her beside her husband. ¹¹ Then great fear came on the whole church and on all who heard these things.

◆ GOING DEEPER

DEUTERONOMY 15:4-6

[4] There will be no poor among you, however, because the LORD is certain to bless you in the land the LORD your God is giving you to possess as an inheritance— [5] if only you obey the LORD your God and are careful to follow every one of these commands I am giving you today. [6] When the LORD your God blesses you as he has promised you, you will lend to many nations but not borrow; you will rule many nations, but they will not rule you.

JOHN 17:20-23

JESUS PRAYS FOR ALL BELIEVERS

[20] "I pray not only for these, but also for those who believe in me through their word. [21] May they all be one, as you, Father, are in me and I am in you. May they also be in us, so that the world may believe you sent me. [22] I have given them the glory you have given me, so that they may be one as we are one. [23] I am in them and you are in me, so that they may be made completely one, that the world may know you have sent me and have loved them as you have loved me."

Notes

Week 1 Reflection

▶ Look over the key themes you marked in this week's readings. What did you notice about the Holy Spirit, the early Church, and the spread of the gospel?

WEEK 1

➤ How do you see these themes at work in your life, community, and local church today?

Grace Day

Take this day to catch up on your reading,
pray, and rest in the presence of the Lord.

"THE ONE WHO BELIEVES IN ME, AS THE

SCRIPTURE HAS SAID, WILL HAVE STREAMS OF

LIVING WATER FLOW FROM DEEP WITHIN HIM."

John 7:83

Notes

Weekly Truth

DAY 7

Scripture is God breathed and true. When we memorize it, we carry the good news of Jesus with us wherever we go.

As we read Acts together, we will memorize a portion of Peter's sermon in Acts 2 that he gave at Pentecost after Jesus's ascension. The apostle called his audience to repent, promising the gift of the Holy Spirit to all who turn to Jesus. This week, let's begin with the first part of verse 37.

DATE

[37] When they heard this, they were pierced to the heart and said to Peter and the rest of the apostles, "Brothers, what should we do?" [38] Peter replied, "Repent and be baptized, each of you, in the name of Jesus Christ for the forgiveness of your sins, and you will receive the gift of the Holy Spirit. [39] For the promise is for you and for your children, and for all who are far off, as many as the Lord our God will call."

Acts 2:37–39

SEE TIPS FOR MEMORIZING SCRIPTURE ON PAGE 196.

The Apostles on Trial Again

DAY 8

Acts 5:12–42; Isaiah 14:24; John 6:66–69

ACTS 5:12–42

APOSTOLIC SIGNS AND WONDERS

[12] Many signs and wonders were being done among the people through the hands of the apostles. They were all together in Solomon's Colonnade. [13] No one else dared to join them, but the people spoke well of them. [14] Believers were added to the Lord in increasing numbers—multitudes of both men and women. [15] As a result, they would carry the sick out into the streets and lay them on cots and mats so that when Peter came by, at least his shadow might fall on some of them. [16] In addition, a multitude came together from the towns surrounding Jerusalem, bringing the sick and those who were tormented by unclean spirits, and they were all healed.

IN AND OUT OF PRISON

[17] Then the high priest rose up. He and all who were with him, who belonged to the party of the Sadducees, were filled with jealousy. [18] So they arrested the apostles and put them in the public jail. [19] But an angel of the Lord opened the doors of the jail during the night, brought them out, and said, [20] "Go and stand in the temple, and tell the people all about this life." [21] Hearing this, they entered the temple at daybreak and began to teach.

THE APOSTLES ON TRIAL AGAIN

When the high priest and those who were with him arrived, they convened the Sanhedrin—the full council of the Israelites—and sent orders to the jail to have them brought. [22] But when the servants got there, they did not find them in the jail; so they returned and reported, [23] "We found the jail securely locked, with the guards standing in front of the doors, but when we opened them, we found no one inside." [24] As the captain of the temple police and the chief priests heard these things, they were baffled about them, wondering what would come of this.

[25] Someone came and reported to them, "Look! The men you put in jail are standing in the temple and teaching the people." [26] Then the commander went with the servants and brought them in without force, because they were afraid the people might stone them. [27] After they brought them in, they had them stand before the Sanhedrin, and the high priest asked, [28] "Didn't we strictly order you not to teach in this name? Look, you have filled Jerusalem with your teaching and are determined to make us guilty of this man's blood."

[29] Peter and the apostles replied, "We must obey God rather than people. [30] The God of our ancestors raised up Jesus, whom you had murdered by hanging him on a tree. [31] God exalted this man to his right hand as ruler and Savior, to give repentance to Israel and forgiveness of sins. [32] We are witnesses of these things, and so is the Holy Spirit whom God has given to those who obey him."

[33] When they heard this, they were enraged and wanted to kill them. [34] But a Pharisee named Gamaliel, a teacher of the law who was respected by all the people, stood up in the Sanhedrin and ordered the men to be taken outside for a little while. [35] He said to them, "Men of Israel, be careful about what you're about to do to these men. [36] Some time ago Theudas rose up, claiming to be somebody, and a group of about four hundred men rallied to him. He was killed, and all his followers were dispersed and came to nothing. [37] After this man, Judas the Galilean rose up in the days of the census and attracted a following. He also perished, and all his followers were scattered. [38] So in the present case, I tell you, stay away from these men and leave them alone. For if this plan or this work is of human origin, it will fail; [39] but if it is of God, you will not be able to overthrow them. You may even be found fighting against God." They were persuaded by him. [40] After they called in the apostles and had them flogged, they ordered them not to speak in the name of Jesus and released them. [41] Then they went out from the presence of the Sanhedrin, rejoicing that they were counted worthy to be treated shamefully on behalf of the Name. [42] Every day in the temple, and in various homes, they continued teaching and proclaiming the good news that Jesus is the Messiah.

◣ GOING DEEPER

ISAIAH 14:24

The LORD of Armies has sworn:

> As I have purposed, so it will be;
> as I have planned it, so it will happen.

JOHN 6:66–69

[66] From that moment many of his disciples turned back and no longer accompanied him. [67] So Jesus said to the Twelve, "You don't want to go away too, do you?"

[68] Simon Peter answered,

"Lord, to whom will we go? You have the words of eternal life.

[69] We have come to believe and know that you are the Holy One of God."

Notes

DATE

THEY WERE UNABLE TO STAND UP AGAINST HIS WISDOM

AND THE SPIRIT BY WHOM HE WAS SPEAKING.

Acts 6:10

Acts 6; Exodus 34:29–30; 1 Timothy 3:8–13

Stephen's Wisdom

ACTS 6

SEVEN CHOSEN TO SERVE

JERUSALEM
AD 34

[1] In those days, as the disciples were increasing in number, there arose a complaint by the Hellenistic Jews against the Hebraic Jews that their widows were being overlooked in the daily distribution. [2] The Twelve summoned the whole company of the disciples and said, "It would not be right for us to give up preaching the word of God to wait on tables. [3] Brothers and sisters, select from among you seven men of good reputation, full of the Spirit and wisdom, whom we can appoint to this duty. [4] But we will devote ourselves to prayer and to the ministry of the word." [5] This proposal pleased the whole company. So they chose Stephen, a man full of faith and the Holy Spirit, and Philip, Prochorus, Nicanor, Timon, Parmenas, and Nicolaus, a convert from Antioch. [6] They had them stand before the apostles, who prayed and laid their hands on them.

[7] So the word of God spread, the disciples in Jerusalem increased greatly in number, and a large group of priests became obedient to the faith.

⁸ Now Stephen, full of grace and power, was performing great wonders and signs among the people.

⁹ Opposition arose, however, from some members of the Freedmen's Synagogue, composed of both Cyrenians and Alexandrians, and some from Cilicia and Asia, and they began to argue with Stephen. ¹⁰ But they were unable to stand up against his wisdom and the Spirit by whom he was speaking.

¹¹ Then they secretly persuaded some men to say, "We heard him speaking blasphemous words against Moses and God." ¹² They stirred up the people, the elders, and the scribes; so they came, seized him, and took him to the Sanhedrin. ¹³ They also presented false witnesses who said, "This man never stops speaking against this holy place and the law. ¹⁴ For we heard him say that this Jesus of Nazareth will destroy this place and change the customs that Moses handed down to us." ¹⁵ And all who were sitting in the Sanhedrin looked intently at him and saw that his face was like the face of an angel.

❤ GOING DEEPER

EXODUS 34:29–30
MOSES'S RADIANT FACE

²⁹ As Moses descended from Mount Sinai—with the two tablets of the testimony in his hands as he descended the mountain—he did not realize that the skin of his face shone as a result of his speaking with the LORD. ³⁰ When Aaron and all the Israelites saw Moses, the skin of his face shone! They were afraid to come near him.

1 TIMOTHY 3:8–13

⁸ Deacons, likewise, should be worthy of respect, not hypocritical, not drinking a lot of wine, not greedy for money, ⁹ holding the mystery of the faith with a clear conscience. ¹⁰ They must also be tested first; if they prove blameless, then they can serve as deacons. ¹¹ Wives, likewise, should be worthy of respect, not slanderers, self-controlled, faithful in everything. ¹² Deacons are to be husbands of one wife, managing their children and their own households competently. ¹³ For those who have served well as deacons acquire a good standing for themselves and great boldness in the faith that is in Christ Jesus.

Notes

DATE

Acts 7; 8:1–3; Psalm 78:1–4; 1 Thessalonians 4:14

Stephen Martyred

**JERUSALEM
AD 34**

ACTS 7

STEPHEN'S SERMON

[1] "Are these things true?" the high priest asked.

[2] "Brothers and fathers," he replied, "listen: The God of glory appeared to our father Abraham when he was in Mesopotamia, before he settled in Haran, [3] and said to him: Leave your country and relatives, and come to the land that I will show you.

[4] "Then he left the land of the Chaldeans and settled in Haran. From there, after his father died, God had him move to this land in which you are now living. [5] He didn't give him an inheritance in it—not even a foot of ground—but he promised to give it to him as a possession, and to his descendants after him, even though he was childless. [6] God spoke in this way: His descendants would be strangers in a foreign country, and they would enslave and oppress them for four hundred years. [7] I will judge the nation that they will serve as slaves, God said. After this, they will come out and worship me in this place. [8] And so he gave Abraham the covenant of circumcision. After this, he fathered Isaac and circumcised him on the eighth day. Isaac became the father of Jacob, and Jacob became the father of the twelve patriarchs.

THE PATRIARCHS IN EGYPT

⁹ "The patriarchs became jealous of Joseph and sold him into Egypt, but God was with him ¹⁰ and rescued him out of all his troubles. He gave him favor and wisdom in the sight of Pharaoh, king of Egypt, who appointed him ruler over Egypt and over his whole household. ¹¹ Now a famine and great suffering came over all of Egypt and Canaan, and our ancestors could find no food. ¹² When Jacob heard there was grain in Egypt, he sent our ancestors there the first time. ¹³ The second time, Joseph revealed himself to his brothers, and Joseph's family became known to Pharaoh. ¹⁴ Joseph invited his father Jacob and all his relatives, seventy-five people in all, ¹⁵ and Jacob went down to Egypt. He and our ancestors died there, ¹⁶ were carried back to Shechem, and were placed in the tomb that Abraham had bought for a sum of silver from the sons of Hamor in Shechem.

MOSES, A REJECTED SAVIOR

¹⁷ "As the time was approaching to fulfill the promise that God had made to Abraham, the people flourished and multiplied in Egypt ¹⁸ until a different king who did not know Joseph ruled over Egypt. ¹⁹ He dealt deceitfully with our race and oppressed our ancestors by making them abandon their infants outside so that they wouldn't survive. ²⁰ At this time Moses was born, and he was beautiful in God's sight. He was cared for in his father's home for three months. ²¹ When he was put outside, Pharaoh's daughter adopted and raised him as her own son. ²² So Moses was educated in all the wisdom of the Egyptians and was powerful in his speech and actions.

²³ "When he was forty years old, he decided to visit his own people, the Israelites. ²⁴ When he saw one of them being mistreated, he came to his rescue and avenged the oppressed man by striking down the Egyptian. ²⁵ He assumed his people would understand that God would give them deliverance through him, but they did not understand. ²⁶ The next day he showed up while they were fighting and tried to reconcile them peacefully, saying, 'Men, you are brothers. Why are you mistreating each other?'

²⁷ "But the one who was mistreating his neighbor pushed Moses aside, saying: Who appointed you a ruler and a judge over us? ²⁸ Do you want to kill me, the same way you killed the Egyptian yesterday?

²⁹ "When he heard this, Moses fled and became an exile in the land of Midian, where he became the father of two sons. ³⁰ After forty years had passed, an angel appeared to him in the wilderness of Mount Sinai, in the flame of a burning bush. ³¹ When Moses saw it, he was amazed at the sight. As he was approaching to look at it, the voice of the Lord came: ³² I am the God of your ancestors—the God of Abraham, of Isaac, and of Jacob. Moses began to tremble and did not dare to look.

³³ "The Lord said to him: Take off the sandals from your feet, because the place where you are standing is holy ground. ³⁴ I have certainly seen the oppression of my people in Egypt; I have heard their groaning and have come down to set them free. And now, come, I will send you to Egypt.

³⁵ "This Moses, whom they rejected when they said, Who appointed you a ruler and a judge?—this one God sent as a ruler and a deliverer through the angel who appeared to him in the bush. ³⁶ This man led them out and performed wonders and signs in the land of Egypt, at the Red Sea, and in the wilderness for forty years.

ISRAEL'S REBELLION AGAINST GOD

³⁷ "This is the Moses who said to the Israelites: God will raise up for you a prophet like me from among your brothers. ³⁸ He is the one who was in the assembly in the wilderness, with the angel who spoke to him on Mount Sinai, and with our ancestors. He received living oracles to give to us. ³⁹ Our ancestors were unwilling to obey him. Instead, they pushed him aside, and in their hearts turned back to Egypt. ⁴⁰ They told Aaron: Make us gods who will go before us. As for this Moses who brought us out of the land of Egypt, we don't know what's happened to him. ⁴¹ They even made a

calf in those days, offered sacrifice to the idol, and were celebrating what their hands had made. [42] God turned away and gave them up to worship the stars of heaven, as it is written in the book of the prophets:

> House of Israel, did you bring me offerings and sacrifices
> for forty years in the wilderness?
> [43] You took up the tent of Moloch
> and the star of your god Rephan,
> the images that you made to worship.
> So I will send you into exile beyond Babylon.

GOD'S REAL TABERNACLE

[44] "Our ancestors had the tabernacle of the testimony in the wilderness, just as he who spoke to Moses commanded him to make it according to the pattern he had seen. [45] Our ancestors in turn received it and with Joshua brought it in when they dispossessed the nations that God drove out before them, until the days of David. [46] He found favor in God's sight and asked that he might provide a dwelling place for the God of Jacob. [47] It was Solomon, rather, who built him a house, [48] but the Most High does not dwell in sanctuaries made with hands, as the prophet says:

> [49] Heaven is my throne,
> and the earth my footstool.
> What sort of house will you build for me?
> says the Lord,
> or what will be my resting place?
> [50] Did not my hand make all these things?

RESISTING THE HOLY SPIRIT

[51] "You stiff-necked people with uncircumcised hearts and ears! You are always resisting the Holy Spirit. As your ancestors did, you do also. [52] Which of the prophets did your ancestors not persecute? They even killed those who foretold the coming of the Righteous One, whose betrayers and murderers you have now become. [53] You received the law under the direction of angels and yet have not kept it."

THE FIRST CHRISTIAN MARTYR

[54] When they heard these things, they were enraged and gnashed their teeth at him. [55] Stephen, full of the Holy Spirit, gazed into heaven. He saw the glory of God, and Jesus standing at the right hand of God. [56] He said,

"Look, I see the heavens opened and the Son of Man standing at the right hand of God!"

[57] They yelled at the top of their voices, covered their ears, and together rushed against him. [58] They dragged him out of the city and began to stone him. And the witnesses laid their garments at the feet of a young man named Saul. [59] While they were stoning Stephen, he called out, "Lord Jesus, receive my spirit!" [60] He knelt down and cried out with a loud voice, "Lord, do not hold this sin against them!" And after saying this, he fell asleep.

ACTS 8:1–3

SAUL THE PERSECUTOR

[1] Saul agreed with putting him to death.

On that day a severe persecution broke out against the church in Jerusalem, and all except the apostles were scattered throughout the land of Judea and Samaria. [2] Devout men buried Stephen and mourned deeply over him. [3] Saul, however, was ravaging the church. He would enter house after house, drag off men and women, and put them in prison.

◆ GOING DEEPER

PSALM 78:1–4

LESSONS FROM ISRAEL'S PAST

A Maskil of Asaph.

[1] My people, hear my instruction;
listen to the words from my mouth.
[2] I will declare wise sayings;
I will speak mysteries from the past—
[3] things we have heard and known
and that our ancestors have passed down to us.
[4] We will not hide them from their children,
but will tell a future generation
the praiseworthy acts of the LORD,
his might, and the wondrous works
he has performed.

1 THESSALONIANS 4:14

For if we believe that Jesus died and rose again, in the same way, through Jesus, God will bring with him those who have fallen asleep.

Key People in Acts

The ministries of Peter and Paul mark the two movements of the gospel to all nations as recorded in Acts. This diagram shows how key people in Acts were connected to both Peter and Paul, as well as to each other.

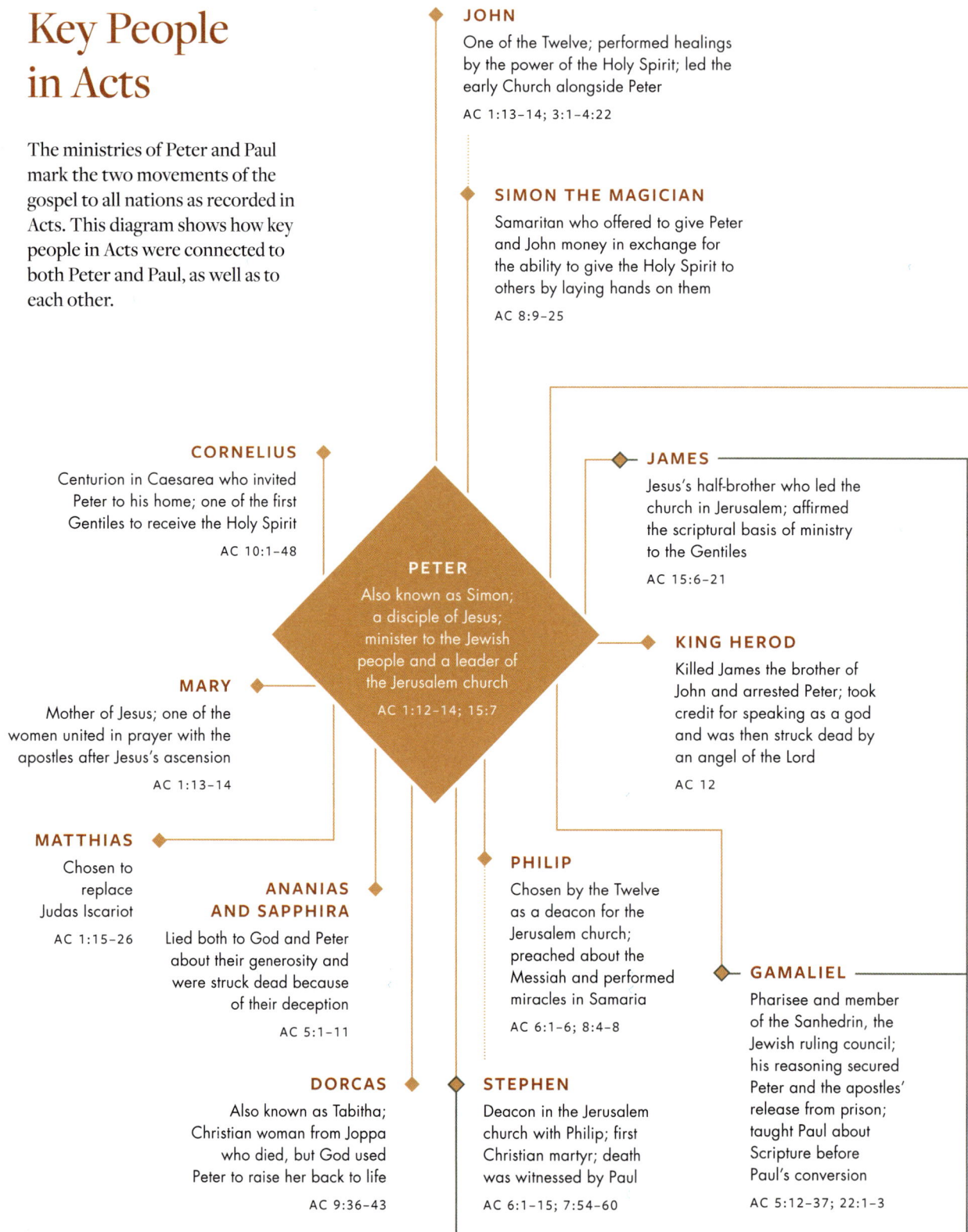

JOHN

One of the Twelve; performed healings by the power of the Holy Spirit; led the early Church alongside Peter

AC 1:13–14; 3:1–4:22

SIMON THE MAGICIAN

Samaritan who offered to give Peter and John money in exchange for the ability to give the Holy Spirit to others by laying hands on them

AC 8:9–25

CORNELIUS

Centurion in Caesarea who invited Peter to his home; one of the first Gentiles to receive the Holy Spirit

AC 10:1–48

JAMES

Jesus's half-brother who led the church in Jerusalem; affirmed the scriptural basis of ministry to the Gentiles

AC 15:6–21

PETER

Also known as Simon; a disciple of Jesus; minister to the Jewish people and a leader of the Jerusalem church

AC 1:12–14; 15:7

KING HEROD

Killed James the brother of John and arrested Peter; took credit for speaking as a god and was then struck dead by an angel of the Lord

AC 12

MARY

Mother of Jesus; one of the women united in prayer with the apostles after Jesus's ascension

AC 1:13–14

MATTHIAS

Chosen to replace Judas Iscariot

AC 1:15–26

ANANIAS AND SAPPHIRA

Lied both to God and Peter about their generosity and were struck dead because of their deception

AC 5:1–11

PHILIP

Chosen by the Twelve as a deacon for the Jerusalem church; preached about the Messiah and performed miracles in Samaria

AC 6:1–6; 8:4–8

GAMALIEL

Pharisee and member of the Sanhedrin, the Jewish ruling council; his reasoning secured Peter and the apostles' release from prison; taught Paul about Scripture before Paul's conversion

AC 5:12–37; 22:1–3

DORCAS

Also known as Tabitha; Christian woman from Joppa who died, but God used Peter to raise her back to life

AC 9:36–43

STEPHEN

Deacon in the Jerusalem church with Philip; first Christian martyr; death was witnessed by Paul

AC 6:1–15; 7:54–60

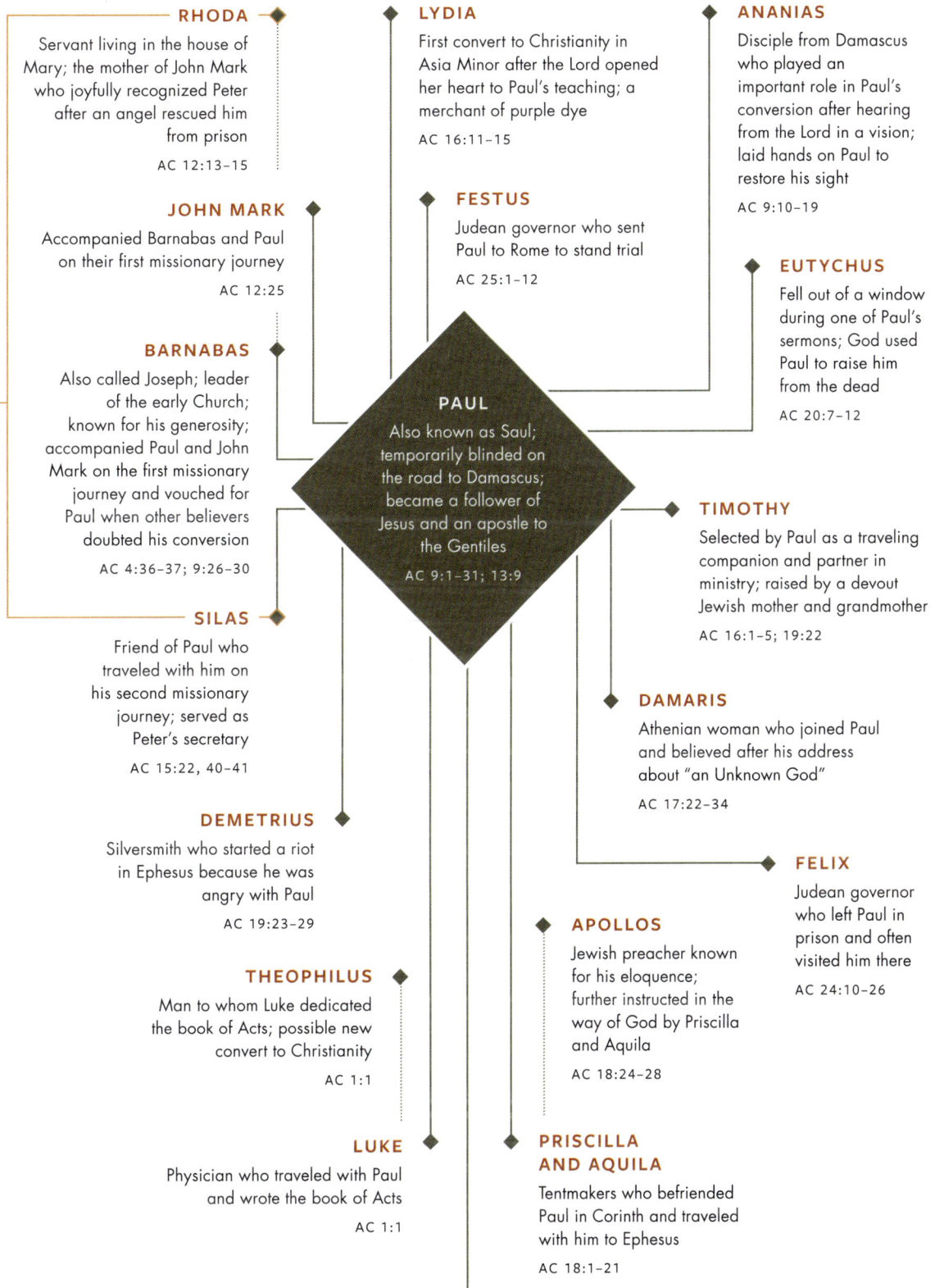

RHODA

Servant living in the house of Mary; the mother of John Mark who joyfully recognized Peter after an angel rescued him from prison

AC 12:13–15

LYDIA

First convert to Christianity in Asia Minor after the Lord opened her heart to Paul's teaching; a merchant of purple dye

AC 16:11–15

ANANIAS

Disciple from Damascus who played an important role in Paul's conversion after hearing from the Lord in a vision; laid hands on Paul to restore his sight

AC 9:10–19

JOHN MARK

Accompanied Barnabas and Paul on their first missionary journey

AC 12:25

FESTUS

Judean governor who sent Paul to Rome to stand trial

AC 25:1–12

EUTYCHUS

Fell out of a window during one of Paul's sermons; God used Paul to raise him from the dead

AC 20:7–12

BARNABAS

Also called Joseph; leader of the early Church; known for his generosity; accompanied Paul and John Mark on the first missionary journey and vouched for Paul when other believers doubted his conversion

AC 4:36–37; 9:26–30

PAUL

Also known as Saul; temporarily blinded on the road to Damascus; became a follower of Jesus and an apostle to the Gentiles

AC 9:1–31; 13:9

TIMOTHY

Selected by Paul as a traveling companion and partner in ministry; raised by a devout Jewish mother and grandmother

AC 16:1–5; 19:22

SILAS

Friend of Paul who traveled with him on his second missionary journey; served as Peter's secretary

AC 15:22, 40–41

DAMARIS

Athenian woman who joined Paul and believed after his address about "an Unknown God"

AC 17:22–34

DEMETRIUS

Silversmith who started a riot in Ephesus because he was angry with Paul

AC 19:23–29

FELIX

Judean governor who left Paul in prison and often visited him there

AC 24:10–26

THEOPHILUS

Man to whom Luke dedicated the book of Acts; possible new convert to Christianity

AC 1:1

APOLLOS

Jewish preacher known for his eloquence; further instructed in the way of God by Priscilla and Aquila

AC 18:24–28

LUKE

Physician who traveled with Paul and wrote the book of Acts

AC 1:1

PRISCILLA AND AQUILA

Tentmakers who befriended Paul in Corinth and traveled with him to Ephesus

AC 18:1–21

Philip proceeded to tell him the good news about Jesus, beginning with that Scripture.

ACTS 8:35

Acts 8:4–40; Isaiah 56:3–5; Romans 10:11–14

Philip and the Ethiopian Official

ACTS 8:4–40

PHILIP IN SAMARIA

JERUSALEM, JUDEA, AND SAMARIA
AD 34

⁴ So those who were scattered went on their way preaching the word. ⁵ Philip went down to a city in Samaria and proclaimed the Messiah to them. ⁶ The crowds were all paying attention to what Philip said, as they listened and saw the signs he was performing. ⁷ For unclean spirits, crying out with a loud voice, came out of many who were possessed, and many who were paralyzed and lame were healed. ⁸ So there was great joy in that city.

THE RESPONSE OF SIMON

⁹ A man named Simon had previously practiced sorcery in that city and amazed the Samaritan people, while claiming to be somebody great. ¹⁰ They all paid attention to him, from the least of them to the greatest, and they said, "This man is called the Great Power of God." ¹¹ They were attentive to him because he had amazed them with his sorceries for a long time. ¹² But when they believed Philip, as he proclaimed the good news about the kingdom of God and the name of Jesus Christ, both men and women were baptized. ¹³ Even Simon himself believed. And after he was baptized, he followed Philip everywhere and was amazed as he observed the signs and great miracles that were being performed.

SIMON'S SIN

¹⁴ When the apostles who were at Jerusalem heard that Samaria had received the word of God, they sent Peter and John to them. ¹⁵ After they went down there,

they prayed for them so that the Samaritans might receive the Holy Spirit because he had not yet come down on any of them. [16] (They had only been baptized in the name of the Lord Jesus.) [17] Then Peter and John laid their hands on them, and they received the Holy Spirit.

[18] When Simon saw that the Spirit was given through the laying on of the apostles' hands, he offered them money, [19] saying, "Give me this power also so that anyone I lay hands on may receive the Holy Spirit."

[20] But Peter told him, "May your silver be destroyed with you, because you thought you could obtain the gift of God with money! [21] You have no part or share in this matter, because your heart is not right before God. [22] Therefore repent of this wickedness of yours, and pray to the Lord that, if possible, your heart's intent may be forgiven. [23] For I see you are poisoned by bitterness and bound by wickedness."

[24] "Pray to the Lord for me," Simon replied, "so that nothing you have said may happen to me."

[25] So, after they had testified and spoken the word of the Lord, they traveled back to Jerusalem, preaching the gospel in many villages of the Samaritans.

THE CONVERSION OF THE ETHIOPIAN OFFICIAL

[26] An angel of the Lord spoke to Philip: "Get up and go south to the road that goes down from Jerusalem to Gaza." (This is the desert road.) [27] So he got up and went. There was an Ethiopian man, a eunuch and high official of Candace, queen of the Ethiopians, who was in charge of her entire treasury. He had come to worship in Jerusalem [28] and was sitting in his chariot on his way home, reading the prophet Isaiah aloud.

[29] The Spirit told Philip, "Go and join that chariot."

[30] When Philip ran up to it, he heard him reading the prophet Isaiah, and said, "Do you understand what you're reading?"

[31] "How can I," he said, "unless someone guides me?" So he invited Philip to come up and sit with him. [32] Now the Scripture passage he was reading was this:

He was led like a sheep to the slaughter,
and as a lamb is silent before its shearer,
so he does not open his mouth.
[33] In his humiliation justice was denied him.
Who will describe his generation?
For his life is taken from the earth.

[34] The eunuch said to Philip, "I ask you, who is the prophet saying this about—himself or someone else?" [35] Philip proceeded to tell him the good news about Jesus, beginning with that Scripture.

[36] As they were traveling down the road, they came to some water.

The eunuch said, "Look, there's water. What would keep me from being baptized?"

[38] So he ordered the chariot to stop, and both Philip and the eunuch went down into the water, and he baptized him. [39] When they came up out of the water, the Spirit of the Lord carried Philip away, and the eunuch did not see him any longer but went on his way rejoicing. [40] Philip appeared in Azotus, and he was traveling and preaching the gospel in all the towns until he came to Caesarea.

🔖 GOING DEEPER

ISAIAH 56:3–5

[3] No foreigner who has joined himself to the LORD should say,
"The LORD will exclude me from his people,"
and the eunuch should not say,
"Look, I am a dried-up tree."
[4] For the LORD says this:
"For the eunuchs who keep my Sabbaths,
and choose what pleases me,
and hold firmly to my covenant,
[5] I will give them, in my house and within my walls,
a memorial and a name
better than sons and daughters.
I will give each of them an everlasting name
that will never be cut off."

ROMANS 10:11-14

[11] For the Scripture says, Everyone who believes on him will not be put to shame, [12] since there is no distinction between Jew and Greek, because the same Lord of all richly blesses all who call on him. [13] For everyone who calls on the name of the Lord will be saved.

ISRAEL'S REJECTION OF THE MESSAGE

[14] How, then, can they call on him they have not believed in? And how can they believe without hearing about him? And how can they hear without a preacher?

Notes

Acts 9:1–31; Psalm 25:8–11; Galatians 1:11–16

Saul's Conversion

▶ **JERUSALEM AND DAMASCUS AD 34–37**

ACTS 9:1–31

THE DAMASCUS ROAD

¹ Now Saul was still breathing threats and murder against the disciples of the Lord. He went to the high priest ² and requested letters from him to the synagogues in Damascus, so that if he found any men or women who belonged to the Way, he might bring them as prisoners to Jerusalem. ³ As he traveled and was nearing Damascus, a light from heaven suddenly flashed around him. ⁴ Falling to the ground, he heard a voice saying to him, "Saul, Saul, why are you persecuting me?"

⁵ "Who are you, Lord?" Saul said.

"I am Jesus, the one you are persecuting," he replied. ⁶ "But get up and go into the city, and you will be told what you must do."

⁷ The men who were traveling with him stood speechless, hearing the sound but seeing no one. ⁸ Saul got up from the ground, and though his eyes were open, he could see nothing. So they took him by the hand and led him into Damascus. ⁹ He was unable to see for three days and did not eat or drink.

SAUL'S BAPTISM

¹⁰ There was a disciple in Damascus named Ananias, and the Lord said to him in a vision, "Ananias."

"Here I am, Lord," he replied.

¹¹ "Get up and go to the street called Straight," the Lord said to him, "to the house of Judas, and ask for a man from Tarsus named Saul, since he is praying there. ¹² In a vision he has seen a man named Ananias coming in and placing his hands on him so that he may regain his sight."

¹³ "Lord," Ananias answered, "I have heard from many people about this man, how much harm he has done to your saints in Jerusalem. ¹⁴ And he has authority here from the chief priests to arrest all who call on your name."

¹⁵ But the Lord said to him,

"Go, for this man is my chosen instrument to take my name to Gentiles, kings, and Israelites.

¹⁶ I will show him how much he must suffer for my name."

¹⁷ Ananias went and entered the house. He placed his hands on him and said, "Brother Saul, the Lord Jesus, who appeared to you on the road you were traveling, has sent me so that you may regain your sight and be filled with the Holy Spirit."

¹⁸ At once something like scales fell from his eyes, and he regained his sight. Then he got up and was baptized. ¹⁹ And after taking some food, he regained his strength.

SAUL PROCLAIMING THE MESSIAH

Saul was with the disciples in Damascus for some time. ²⁰ Immediately he began proclaiming Jesus in the synagogues: "He is the Son of God."

²¹ All who heard him were astounded and said, "Isn't this the man in Jerusalem who was causing havoc for those who called on this name and came here for the purpose of taking them as prisoners to the chief priests?"

²² But Saul grew stronger and kept confounding the Jews who lived in Damascus by proving that Jesus is the Messiah.

²³ After many days had passed, the Jews conspired to kill him, ²⁴ but Saul learned of their plot. So they were watching the gates day and night intending to kill him, ²⁵ but his disciples took him by night and lowered him in a large basket through an opening in the wall.

SAUL IN JERUSALEM

²⁶ When he arrived in Jerusalem, he tried to join the disciples, but they were all afraid of him, since they did not believe he was a disciple. ²⁷ Barnabas, however,

took him and brought him to the apostles and explained to them how Saul had seen the Lord on the road and that the Lord had talked to him, and how in Damascus he had spoken boldly in the name of Jesus. [28] Saul was coming and going with them in Jerusalem, speaking boldly in the name of the Lord. [29] He conversed and debated with the Hellenistic Jews, but they tried to kill him. [30] When the brothers found out, they took him down to Caesarea and sent him off to Tarsus.

THE CHURCH'S GROWTH

[31] So the church throughout all Judea, Galilee, and Samaria had peace and was strengthened. Living in the fear of the Lord and encouraged by the Holy Spirit, it increased in numbers.

◆ GOING DEEPER

PSALM 25:8–11

[8] The LORD is good and upright;
therefore he shows sinners the way.
[9] He leads the humble in what is right
and teaches them his way.
[10] All the LORD's ways show faithful love and truth
to those who keep his covenant and decrees.
[11] LORD, for the sake of your name,
forgive my iniquity, for it is immense.

GALATIANS 1:11–16

THE ORIGIN OF PAUL'S GOSPEL

[11] For I want you to know, brothers and sisters, that the gospel preached by me is not of human origin. [12] For I did not receive it from a human source and I was not taught it, but it came by a revelation of Jesus Christ.

[13] For you have heard about my former way of life in Judaism: I intensely persecuted God's church and tried to destroy it. [14] I advanced in Judaism beyond many contemporaries among my people, because I was extremely zealous for the traditions of my ancestors. [15] But when God, who from my mother's womb set me apart and called me by his grace, was pleased [16] to reveal his Son in me, so that I could preach him among the Gentiles, I did not immediately consult with anyone.

Notes

Week 2 Reflection

> Look over the key themes you marked in this week's readings. What did you notice about the Holy Spirit, the early Church, and the spread of the gospel?

▶ How do you see these themes at work in your life, community, and local church today?

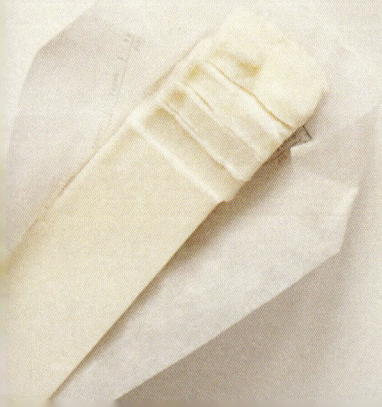

Cast-Iron Cornbread

PREP TIME
10 minutes

COOK TIME
20–25 minutes

SERVES
8

INGREDIENTS

1½ cups self-rising cornmeal

½ cup vegetable oil

1 cup sharp cheddar cheese, grated

1 medium onion, diced

3 tablespoons hot peppers, chopped

1 (11-ounce) can southwest corn

1 cup whole milk

2 eggs, beaten

1 teaspoon salt

INSTRUCTIONS

Place a 7-inch cast-iron skillet in oven. Preheat to 400°F, heating skillet in oven as it warms.

Stir ingredients together until combined.

Remove skillet from oven, grease if necessary, then pour batter into hot skillet. Bake for 20 to 25 minutes, or until lightly golden brown and baked through.

Let cool in skillet for 10 minutes before serving.

Grace Day

Take this day to catch up on your reading,
pray, and rest in the presence of the Lord.

FOR THE SCRIPTURE SAYS, EVERYONE WHO

BELIEVES ON HIM WILL NOT BE PUT TO SHAME...

Romans 10:11

Notes

Weekly Truth

DAY 14

Scripture is God breathed and true. When we memorize it, we carry the good news of Jesus with us wherever we go.

As we read Acts together, we are memorizing a portion of Peter's sermon in Acts 2. This week, memorize all of verse 37.

DATE

[37] When they heard this, they were pierced to the heart and said to Peter and the rest of the apostles, "Brothers, what should we do?" [38] Peter replied, "Repent and be baptized, each of you, in the name of Jesus Christ for the forgiveness of your sins, and you will receive the gift of the Holy Spirit. [39] For the promise is for you and for your children, and for all who are far off, as many as the Lord our God will call."

Acts 2:37–39

SEE TIPS FOR MEMORIZING SCRIPTURE ON PAGE 196.

HE KNELT DOWN, PRAYED, AND TURNING TOWARD

THE BODY SAID, "TABITHA, GET UP."

Acts 9:40

Acts 9:32–43; Psalm 36:9; Mark 5:21–43

Dorcas Restored to Life

ACTS 9:32–43

THE HEALING OF AENEAS

▶ LYDDA AND JOPPA
AD 39

[32] As Peter was traveling from place to place, he also came down to the saints who lived in Lydda. [33] There he found a man named Aeneas, who was paralyzed and had been bedridden for eight years. [34] Peter said to him, "Aeneas, Jesus Christ heals you. Get up and make your bed," and immediately he got up. [35] So all who lived in Lydda and Sharon saw him and turned to the Lord.

DORCAS RESTORED TO LIFE

[36] In Joppa there was a disciple named Tabitha (which is translated Dorcas). She was always doing good works and acts of charity. [37] About that time she became sick and died. After washing her, they placed her in a room upstairs. [38] Since Lydda was near Joppa, the disciples heard that Peter was there and sent two men to him who urged him, "Don't delay in coming with us." [39] Peter got up and went with them. When he arrived, they led him to the room upstairs. And all the widows approached him, weeping and showing him the robes and clothes that Dorcas had made while she was with them. [40] Peter sent them all out of the room. He knelt down, prayed, and turning toward the body said, "Tabitha, get

up." She opened her eyes, saw Peter, and sat up. ⁴¹ He gave her his hand and helped her stand up. He called the saints and widows and presented her alive. ⁴² This became known throughout Joppa, and many believed in the Lord. ⁴³ Peter stayed for some time in Joppa with Simon, a leather tanner.

♥ GOING DEEPER

PSALM 36:9

For the wellspring of life is with you.
By means of your light we see light.

MARK 5:21-43

A GIRL RESTORED AND A WOMAN HEALED

²¹ When Jesus had crossed over again by boat to the other side, a large crowd gathered around him while he was by the sea. ²² One of the synagogue leaders, named Jairus, came, and when he saw Jesus, he fell at his feet ²³ and begged him earnestly, "My little daughter is dying. Come and lay your hands on her so that she can get well and live." ²⁴ So Jesus went with him, and a large crowd was following and pressing against him.

²⁵ Now a woman suffering from bleeding for twelve years ²⁶ had endured much under many doctors. She had spent everything she had and was not helped at all. On the contrary, she became worse. ²⁷ Having heard about Jesus, she came up behind him in the crowd and touched his clothing. ²⁸ For she said, "If I just touch his clothes, I'll be made well." ²⁹ Instantly her flow of blood ceased, and she sensed in her body that she was healed of her affliction.

³⁰ Immediately Jesus realized that power had gone out from him. He turned around in the crowd and said, "Who touched my clothes?"

³¹ His disciples said to him, "You see the crowd pressing against you, and yet you say, 'Who touched me?'"

³² But he was looking around to see who had done this. ³³ The woman, with fear and trembling, knowing what had happened to her, came and fell down before him, and told him the whole truth. ³⁴ "Daughter," he said to her, "your faith has saved you. Go in peace and be healed from your affliction."

³⁵ While he was still speaking, people came from the synagogue leader's house and said, "Your daughter is dead. Why bother the teacher anymore?"

³⁶ When Jesus overheard what was said, he told the synagogue leader, "Don't be afraid. Only believe." ³⁷ He did not let anyone accompany him except Peter, James, and John, James's brother. ³⁸ They came to the leader's house, and he saw a commotion—people weeping and wailing loudly. ³⁹ He went in and said to them, "Why are you making a commotion and weeping? The child is not dead but asleep." ⁴⁰ They laughed at him, but he put them all outside. He took the child's father, mother, and those who were with him, and entered the place where the child was. ⁴¹ Then he took the child by the hand and said to her, *"Talitha koum"* (which is translated, "Little girl, I say to you, get up"). ⁴² Immediately the girl got up and began to walk. (She was twelve years old.) At this they were utterly astounded. ⁴³ Then he gave them strict orders that no one should know about this and told them to give her something to eat.

Notes

DATE

Good News for Gentiles

DAY 16

Acts 10; Isaiah 52:7–10; Galatians 3:27–28

ACTS 10

CORNELIUS'S VISION

¹ There was a man in Caesarea named Cornelius, a centurion of what was called the Italian Regiment. ² He was a devout man and feared God along with his whole household. He did many charitable deeds for the Jewish people and always prayed to God. ³ About three in the afternoon he distinctly saw in a vision an angel of God who came in and said to him, "Cornelius."

⁴ Staring at him in awe, he said, "What is it, Lord?"

The angel told him, "Your prayers and your acts of charity have ascended as a memorial offering before God. ⁵ Now send men to Joppa and call for Simon, who is also named Peter. ⁶ He is lodging with Simon, a tanner, whose house is by the sea."

⁷ When the angel who spoke to him had gone, he called two of his household servants and a devout soldier, who was one of those who attended him. ⁸ After explaining everything to them, he sent them to Joppa.

PETER'S VISION

⁹ The next day, as they were traveling and nearing the city, Peter went up to pray on the roof about noon. ¹⁰ He became hungry and wanted to eat, but while they were preparing something, he fell into a trance. ¹¹ He saw heaven opened and an object that resembled a large sheet coming down, being lowered by its four corners to the earth. ¹² In it were all the four-footed animals and reptiles of the earth, and the birds of the sky. ¹³ A voice said to him, "Get up, Peter; kill and eat."

¹⁴ "No, Lord!" Peter said. "For I have never eaten anything impure and ritually unclean."

¹⁵ Again, a second time, the voice said to him, "What God has made clean, do not call impure." ¹⁶ This happened three times, and suddenly the object was taken up into heaven.

PETER VISITS CORNELIUS

¹⁷ While Peter was deeply perplexed about what the vision he had seen might mean, right away the men who had been sent by Cornelius, having asked directions to Simon's house, stood at the gate. ¹⁸ They called out, asking if Simon, who was also named Peter, was lodging there.

¹⁹ While Peter was thinking about the vision, the Spirit told him, "Three men are here looking for you. ²⁰ Get up, go downstairs, and go with them with no doubts at all, because I have sent them."

²¹ Then Peter went down to the men and said, "Here I am, the one you're looking for. What is the reason you're here?"

²² They said, "Cornelius, a centurion, an upright and God-fearing man, who has a good reputation with the whole Jewish nation, was divinely directed by a holy angel to call you to his house and to hear a message from you." ²³ Peter then invited them in and gave them lodging.

The next day he got up and set out with them, and some of the brothers from Joppa went with him. ²⁴ The following day he entered Caesarea. Now Cornelius was expecting them and had called together his relatives and close friends. ²⁵ When Peter entered, Cornelius met him, fell at his feet, and worshiped him.

²⁶ But Peter lifted him up and said, "Stand up. I myself am also a man." ²⁷ While talking with him, he went in and found a large gathering of people. ²⁸ Peter said to them, "You know it's forbidden for a Jewish man to associate with or visit a foreigner, but God has shown me that I must not call any person impure or unclean. ²⁹ That's why I came without any objection when I was sent for. So may I ask why you sent for me?"

³⁰ Cornelius replied, "Four days ago at this hour, at three in the afternoon, I was praying in my house. Just then a man in dazzling clothing stood before me ³¹ and said, 'Cornelius, your prayer has been heard, and your acts of charity have been remembered in God's sight. ³² Therefore send someone to Joppa and invite Simon here, who is also named Peter. He is lodging in Simon the tanner's house by the sea.' ³³ So I immediately sent for you, and it was good of you to come. So now we are all in the presence of God to hear everything you have been commanded by the Lord."

GOOD NEWS FOR GENTILES

³⁴ Peter began to speak:

"Now I truly understand that God doesn't show favoritism, ³⁵ but in every nation the person who fears him and does what is right is acceptable to him.

³⁶ He sent the message to the Israelites, proclaiming the good news of peace through Jesus Christ—he is Lord of all. ³⁷ You know the events that took place throughout all Judea, beginning from Galilee after the baptism that John preached: ³⁸ how God anointed Jesus of Nazareth with the Holy Spirit and with power, and how he went about doing good and healing all who were under the tyranny of the devil, because God was with him. ³⁹ We ourselves are witnesses of everything he did in both the Judean country and in Jerusalem, and yet they killed him by hanging him on a tree. ⁴⁰ God raised up this man on the third day and caused him to be seen, ⁴¹ not by all the people, but by us whom God appointed as witnesses, who ate and drank with him after he rose from the dead. ⁴² He commanded us to preach to the people and to testify that he is the one appointed by God to be the judge of the living and the dead. ⁴³ All the prophets testify about him that through his name everyone who believes in him receives forgiveness of sins."

GENTILE CONVERSION AND BAPTISM

⁴⁴ While Peter was still speaking these words, the Holy Spirit came down on all those who heard the message. ⁴⁵ The circumcised believers who had come with Peter were amazed because the gift of the Holy Spirit had been poured out even on the Gentiles. ⁴⁶ For they heard them speaking in tongues and declaring the greatness of God.

Then Peter responded, ⁴⁷ "Can anyone withhold water and prevent these people from being baptized, who have received the Holy Spirit just as we have?" ⁴⁸ He commanded them to be baptized in the name of Jesus Christ. Then they asked him to stay for a few days.

◆ GOING DEEPER

ISAIAH 52:7-10

⁷ How beautiful on the mountains
are the feet of the herald,
who proclaims peace,
who brings news of good things,
who proclaims salvation,
who says to Zion, "Your God reigns!"

8 The voices of your watchmen—
they lift up their voices,
shouting for joy together;
for every eye will see
when the LORD returns to Zion.
9 Be joyful, rejoice together,
you ruins of Jerusalem!
For the LORD has comforted his people;
he has redeemed Jerusalem.
10 The LORD has displayed his holy arm
in the sight of all the nations;
all the ends of the earth will see
the salvation of our God.

GALATIANS 3:27–28

27 For those of you who were baptized into Christ have been clothed with Christ. 28 There is no Jew or Greek, slave or free, male and female; since you are all one in Christ Jesus.

Acts 11; Hebrews 13:15–16; 1 Peter 4:16–19

The Church in Antioch

**JERUSALEM AND
SYRIAN ANTIOCH
AD 41–44**

ACTS 11

GENTILE SALVATION DEFENDED

[1] The apostles and the brothers and sisters who were throughout Judea heard that the Gentiles had also received the word of God. [2] When Peter went up to Jerusalem, the circumcision party criticized him, [3] saying, "You went to uncircumcised men and ate with them."

[4] Peter began to explain to them step by step, [5] "I was in the town of Joppa praying, and I saw, in a trance, an object that resembled a large sheet coming down, being lowered by its four corners from heaven, and it came to me. [6] When I looked closely and considered it, I saw the four-footed animals of the earth, the wild beasts, the reptiles, and the birds of the sky. [7] I also heard a voice telling me, 'Get up, Peter; kill and eat.'

[8] "'No, Lord!' I said. 'For nothing impure or ritually unclean has ever entered my mouth.' [9] But a voice answered from heaven a second time, 'What God has made clean, you must not call impure.'

[10] "Now this happened three times, and everything was drawn up again into heaven. [11] At that very moment, three men who had been sent to me from Caesarea arrived at the house where we were. [12] The Spirit told me to accompany them with no doubts at all. These six brothers also accompanied me, and we went into the

man's house. ¹³ He reported to us how he had seen the angel standing in his house and saying, 'Send to Joppa, and call for Simon, who is also named Peter. ¹⁴ He will speak a message to you by which you and all your household will be saved.'

¹⁵ "As I began to speak, the Holy Spirit came down on them, just as on us at the beginning. ¹⁶ I remembered the word of the Lord, how he said, 'John baptized with water, but you will be baptized with the Holy Spirit.' ¹⁷ If, then, God gave them the same gift that he also gave to us when we believed in the Lord Jesus Christ, how could I possibly hinder God?"

¹⁸ When they heard this they became silent. And they glorified God, saying, "So then, God has given repentance resulting in life even to the Gentiles."

THE CHURCH IN ANTIOCH

¹⁹ Now those who had been scattered as a result of the persecution that started because of Stephen made their way as far as Phoenicia, Cyprus, and Antioch, speaking the word to no one except Jews. ²⁰ But there were some of them, men from Cyprus and Cyrene, who came to Antioch and began speaking to the Greeks also, proclaiming the good news about the Lord Jesus. ²¹ The Lord's hand was with them, and a large number who believed turned to the Lord. ²² News about them reached the church in Jerusalem, and they sent out Barnabas to travel as far as Antioch.

²³ When he arrived and saw the grace of God, he was glad and encouraged all of them to remain true to the Lord with devoted hearts,

²⁴ for he was a good man, full of the Holy Spirit and of faith. And large numbers of people were added to the Lord.

²⁵ Then he went to Tarsus to search for Saul, ²⁶ and when he found him he brought him to Antioch. For a whole year they met with the church and taught large numbers. The disciples were first called Christians at Antioch.

FAMINE RELIEF

²⁷ In those days some prophets came down from Jerusalem to Antioch. ²⁸ One of them, named Agabus, stood up and predicted by the Spirit that there would be a severe famine throughout the Roman world. This took place during the reign of Claudius. ²⁹ Each of the disciples, according to his ability, determined to send relief to the brothers and sisters who lived in Judea. ³⁰ They did this, sending it to the elders by means of Barnabas and Saul.

🛡 GOING DEEPER

HEBREWS 13:15–16

¹⁵ Therefore, through him let us continually offer up to God a sacrifice of praise, that is, the fruit of lips that confess his name. ¹⁶ Don't neglect to do what is good and to share, for God is pleased with such sacrifices

1 PETER 4:16–19

¹⁶ But if anyone suffers as a Christian, let him not be ashamed but let him glorify God in having that name. ¹⁷ For the time has come for judgment to begin with God's household, and if it begins with us, what will the outcome be for those who disobey the gospel of God?

¹⁸ And if a righteous person is saved with difficulty,
what will become of the ungodly and the sinner?

¹⁹ So then, let those who suffer according to God's will entrust themselves to a faithful Creator while doing what is good.

Notes

DATE

What Is the Church?

Acts records the widespread growth of early faith communities and offers historical context for the active, global Church we are part of today. Throughout the New Testament, different metaphors for the Church are used to help us understand what this community of believers is and how it is meant to function. Included here are some of the images used in the New Testament to describe the Church.

THE BODY OF CHRIST

As it is, there are many parts, but one body. 1CO 12:20

Now you are the body of Christ, and individual members of it. 1CO 12:27

To equip the saints for the work of ministry, to build up the body of Christ. EPH 4:12

He is also the head of the body, the church. COL 1:18

THE BRIDE OF CHRIST

I have promised you in marriage to one husband—to present a pure virgin to Christ. 2CO 11:2

Husbands, love your wives, just as Christ loved the church and gave himself for her to make her holy... EPH 5:25–26

The marriage of the Lamb has come, and his bride has prepared herself. RV 19:7

THE FAMILY OF GOD

"Whoever does the will of my Father in heaven is my brother and sister and mother." MT 12:50

We are God's children, and if children, also heirs—heirs of God and coheirs with Christ. RM 8:16–17

"And I will be a Father to you, and you will be sons and daughters to me." 2CO 6:18

Let us work for the good of all, especially for those who belong to the household of faith. GL 6:10

See what great love the Father has given us that we should be called God's children—and we are! 1JN 3:1

THE FLOCK

"Don't be afraid, little flock, because your Father delights to give you the kingdom." LK 12:32

"I am the good shepherd. The good shepherd lays down his life for the sheep." JN 10:11

Be on guard for yourselves and for all the flock of which the Holy Spirit has appointed you as overseers, to shepherd the church of God. AC 20:28

Our Lord Jesus—the great Shepherd of the sheep... HEB 13:20

THE HOUSE OF GOD / CHRIST	You are no longer foreigners and strangers, but fellow citizens with the saints, and members of God's household. EPH 2:19
	…God's household, which is the church of the living God, the pillar and foundation of the truth. 1TM 3:15
	Christ was faithful as a Son over his household. And we are that household… HEB 3:6
	You yourselves, as living stones, a spiritual house, are being built to be a holy priesthood. 1PT 2:5
THE LAMPSTAND / THE LIGHT OF THE WORLD	"You are the light of the world. A city situated on a hill cannot be hidden." MT 5:14
	"…the seven lampstands are the seven churches." RV 1:20
THE LETTERS	You show that you are Christ's letter, delivered by us, not written with ink but with the Spirit of the living God—not on tablets of stone but on tablets of human hearts. 2CO 3:3
THE PEOPLE OF GOD	Our citizenship is in heaven. PHP 3:20
	But you are a chosen race, a royal priesthood, a holy nation, a people for his possession… 1PT 2:9
	…and made us a kingdom, priests to his God and Father… RV 1:6
	They will be his peoples, and God himself will be with them and will be their God. RV 21:3
THE TEMPLE OF THE SPIRIT	Don't you yourselves know that you are God's temple and that the Spirit of God lives in you? 1CO 3:16
	For we are the temple of the living God. 2CO 6:16
	In him you are also being built together for God's dwelling in the Spirit. EPH 2:22

SO PETER WAS KEPT IN PRISON, BUT THE CHURCH

WAS PRAYING FERVENTLY TO GOD FOR HIM.

Acts 12:5

Acts 12:1–25, Daniel 3:28–30, Ephesians 6:19–20

Peter Rescued by an Angel

ACTS 12

JAMES MARTYRED AND PETER JAILED

JERUSALEM, JUDEA, AND CAESAREA MARITIMA AD 44–47

[1] About that time King Herod violently attacked some who belonged to the church, [2] and he executed James, John's brother, with the sword. [3] When he saw that it pleased the Jews, he proceeded to arrest Peter too, during the Festival of Unleavened Bread. [4] After the arrest, he put him in prison and assigned four squads of four soldiers each to guard him, intending to bring him out to the people after the Passover. [5] So Peter was kept in prison, but the church was praying fervently to God for him.

PETER RESCUED

[6] When Herod was about to bring him out for trial, that very night Peter, bound with two chains, was sleeping between two soldiers, while the sentries in front of the door guarded the prison. [7] Suddenly an angel of the Lord appeared, and a light shone in the cell. Striking Peter on the side, he woke him up and said, "Quick, get up!" And the chains fell off his wrists. [8] "Get dressed," the angel told him, "and put on your sandals." And he did. "Wrap your cloak around you," he told him, "and follow me." [9] So he went out and followed, and he did not know that what the angel did was really happening, but he thought he was seeing a vision. [10] After they passed the first and second guards, they came to the iron gate that leads into the city, which opened to them by itself. They went outside and passed one street, and suddenly the angel left him.

¹¹ When Peter came to himself, he said, "Now I know for certain that the Lord has sent his angel and rescued me from Herod's grasp and from all that the Jewish people expected." ¹² As soon as he realized this, he went to the house of Mary, the mother of John who was called Mark, where many had assembled and were praying. ¹³ He knocked at the door of the outer gate, and a servant named Rhoda came to answer. ¹⁴ She recognized Peter's voice, and because of her joy, she did not open the gate but ran in and announced that Peter was standing at the outer gate.

¹⁵ "You're out of your mind!" they told her. But she kept insisting that it was true, and they said, "It's his angel." ¹⁶ Peter, however, kept on knocking, and when they opened the door and saw him, they were amazed.

¹⁷ Motioning to them with his hand to be silent, he described to them how the Lord had brought him out of the prison. "Tell these things to James and the brothers," he said, and he left and went to another place.

¹⁸ At daylight, there was a great commotion among the soldiers as to what had become of Peter. ¹⁹ After Herod had searched and did not find him, he interrogated the guards and ordered their execution. Then Herod went down from Judea to Caesarea and stayed there.

HEROD'S DEATH

²⁰ Herod had been very angry with the people of Tyre and Sidon. Together they presented themselves before him. After winning over Blastus, who was in charge of the king's bedroom, they asked for peace, because their country was supplied with food from the king's country. ²¹ On an appointed day, dressed in royal robes and seated on the throne, Herod delivered a speech to them. ²² The assembled people began to shout, "It's the voice of a god and not of a man!" ²³ At once an angel of the Lord struck him because he did not give the glory to God, and he was eaten by worms and died.

²⁴ But the word of God spread and multiplied.

²⁵ After they had completed their relief mission, Barnabas and Saul returned to Jerusalem, taking along John who was called Mark.

◆ GOING DEEPER

DANIEL 3:28–30

²⁸ Nebuchadnezzar exclaimed, "Praise to the God of Shadrach, Meshach, and Abednego! He sent his angel and rescued his servants who trusted in him. They violated the king's command and risked their lives rather than serve or worship any god except their own God. ²⁹ Therefore I issue a decree that anyone of any people, nation, or language who says anything offensive against the God of Shadrach, Meshach, and Abednego will be torn limb from limb and his house made a garbage dump. For there is no other god who is able to deliver like this." ³⁰ Then the king rewarded Shadrach, Meshach, and Abednego in the province of Babylon.

EPHESIANS 6:19–20

¹⁹ Pray also for me, that the message may be given to me when I open my mouth to make known with boldness the mystery of the gospel. ²⁰ For this I am an ambassador in chains. Pray that I might be bold enough to speak about it as I should.

Notes

DATE

Acts 13; Isaiah 49:6; Galatians 2:15–21

Preparing for the Mission Field

SYRIAN ANTIOCH, CYPRUS, AND PISIDIAN ANTIOCH AD 47

ACTS 13

PREPARING FOR THE MISSION FIELD

¹ Now in the church at Antioch there were prophets and teachers: Barnabas, Simeon who was called Niger, Lucius of Cyrene, Manaen, a close friend of Herod the tetrarch, and Saul.

² As they were worshiping the Lord and fasting, the Holy Spirit said, "Set apart for me Barnabas and Saul for the work to which I have called them." ³ Then after they had fasted, prayed, and laid hands on them, they sent them off.

THE MISSION TO CYPRUS

⁴ So being sent out by the Holy Spirit, they went down to Seleucia, and from there they sailed to Cyprus. ⁵ Arriving in Salamis, they proclaimed the word of God in the Jewish synagogues. They also had John as their assistant. ⁶ When they had traveled the whole island as far as Paphos, they came across a sorcerer, a Jewish false prophet named Bar-Jesus. ⁷ He was with the proconsul, Sergius Paulus, an intelligent man. This man summoned Barnabas and Saul and wanted to hear the word of God. ⁸ But Elymas the sorcerer (that is the meaning of his name) opposed them and tried to turn the proconsul away from the faith.

⁹ But Saul—also called Paul—filled with the Holy Spirit, stared straight at Elymas ¹⁰ and said, "You are full of all kinds of deceit and trickery, you son of the devil

and enemy of all that is right. Won't you ever stop perverting the straight paths of the Lord? [11] Now, look, the Lord's hand is against you. You are going to be blind, and will not see the sun for a time." Immediately a mist and darkness fell on him, and he went around seeking someone to lead him by the hand.

[12] Then, when he saw what happened, the proconsul believed, because he was astonished at the teaching of the Lord.

PAUL'S SERMON IN ANTIOCH OF PISIDIA

[13] Paul and his companions set sail from Paphos and came to Perga in Pamphylia, but John left them and went back to Jerusalem. [14] They continued their journey from Perga and reached Pisidian Antioch. On the Sabbath day they went into the synagogue and sat down. [15] After the reading of the Law and the Prophets, the leaders of the synagogue sent word to them, saying, "Brothers, if you have any word of encouragement for the people, you can speak."

[16] Paul stood up and motioned with his hand and said, "Fellow Israelites, and you who fear God, listen! [17] The God of this people Israel chose our ancestors, made the people prosper during their stay in the land of Egypt, and led them out of it with a mighty arm. [18] And for about forty years he put up with them in the wilderness; [19] and after destroying seven nations in the land of Canaan, he gave them their land as an inheritance. [20] This all took about 450 years. After this, he gave them judges until Samuel the prophet. [21] Then they asked for a king, and God gave them Saul the son of Kish, a man of the tribe of Benjamin, for forty years. [22] After removing him, he raised up David as their king and testified about him, 'I have found David the son of Jesse to be a man after my own heart, who will carry out all my will.'

[23] "From this man's descendants, as he promised, God brought to Israel the Savior, Jesus. [24] Before his coming to public attention, John had previously proclaimed a baptism of repentance to all the people of Israel. [25] Now as John was completing his mission, he said, 'Who do you think I am? I am not the one. But one is coming after me, and I am not worthy to untie the sandals on his feet.'

[26] "Brothers and sisters, children of Abraham's race, and those among you who fear God, it is to us that the word of this salvation has been sent. [27] Since the residents of Jerusalem and their rulers did not recognize him or the sayings of the prophets that are read every Sabbath, they have fulfilled their words by condemning him. [28] Though they found no grounds for the death sentence, they asked Pilate to have him killed. [29] When they had carried out all that had been written about him, they took him down from the tree and put him in a tomb. [30] But God raised him from the dead, [31] and he appeared for many days to those who came up with him from Galilee to Jerusalem, who are now his witnesses to the people. [32] And we ourselves proclaim to you the good news of the promise that was made to our ancestors. [33] God has fulfilled this for us, their children, by raising up Jesus, as it is written in the second Psalm:

> You are my Son;
> today I have become your Father.

[34] As to his raising him from the dead, never to return to decay, he has spoken in this way, I will give you the holy and sure promises of David. [35] Therefore he also says in another passage, You will not let your Holy One see decay. [36] For David, after serving God's purpose in his own generation, fell asleep, was buried with his fathers, and decayed, [37] but the one God raised up did not decay.

[38] Therefore, let it be known to you, brothers and sisters, that through this man forgiveness of sins is being proclaimed to you.

[39] Everyone who believes is justified through him from everything that you could not be justified from through the law of Moses. [40] So beware that what is said in the prophets does not happen to you:

> [41] Look, you scoffers,
> marvel and vanish away,
> because I am doing a work in your days,
> a work that you will never believe,
> even if someone were to explain it to you."

42 As they were leaving, the people urged them to speak about these matters the following Sabbath. 43 After the synagogue had been dismissed, many of the Jews and devout converts to Judaism followed Paul and Barnabas, who were speaking with them and urging them to continue in the grace of God.

44 The following Sabbath almost the whole town assembled to hear the word of the Lord. 45 But when the Jews saw the crowds, they were filled with jealousy and began to contradict what Paul was saying, insulting him.

46 Paul and Barnabas boldly replied, "It was necessary that the word of God be spoken to you first. Since you reject it and judge yourselves unworthy of eternal life, we are turning to the Gentiles. 47 For this is what the Lord has commanded us:

I have made you
a light for the Gentiles
to bring salvation
to the ends of the earth."

48 When the Gentiles heard this, they rejoiced and honored the word of the Lord, and all who had been appointed to eternal life believed. 49 The word of the Lord spread through the whole region. 50 But the Jews incited the prominent God-fearing women and the leading men of the city. They stirred up persecution against Paul and Barnabas and expelled them from their district. 51 But Paul and Barnabas shook the dust off their feet against them and went to Iconium. 52 And the disciples were filled with joy and the Holy Spirit.

ISAIAH 49:6

He says,
"It is not enough for you to be my servant
raising up the tribes of Jacob
and restoring the protected ones of Israel.
I will also make you a light for the nations,
to be my salvation to the ends of the earth."

GALATIANS 2:15–21

15 We are Jews by birth and not "Gentile sinners," 16 and yet because we know that a person is not justified by the works of the law but by faith in Jesus Christ, even we ourselves have believed in Christ Jesus. This was so that we might be justified by faith in Christ and not by the works of the law, because by the works of the law no human being will be justified. 17 But if we ourselves are also found to be "sinners" while seeking to be justified by Christ, is Christ then a promoter of sin? Absolutely not! 18 If I rebuild those things that I tore down, I show myself to be a lawbreaker. 19 For through the law I died to the law, so that I might live for God. 20 I have been crucified with Christ, and I no longer live, but Christ lives in me. The life I now live in the body, I live by faith in the Son of God, who loved me and gave himself for me. 21 I do not set aside the grace of God, for if righteousness comes through the law, then Christ died for nothing.

Notes

DATE

Week 3 Reflection

> Look over the key themes you marked in this week's readings. What did you notice about the Holy Spirit, the early Church, and the spread of the gospel?

> How do you see these themes at work in your life, community, and local church today?

Grace Day

Take this day to catch up on your reading,
pray, and rest in the presence of the Lord.

HOW BEAUTIFUL ON THE MOUNTAINS ARE THE FEET

OF THE HERALD, WHO PROCLAIMS PEACE, WHO

BRINGS NEWS OF GOOD THINGS, WHO PROCLAIMS

SALVATION, WHO SAYS TO ZION, "YOUR GOD REIGNS!"

Isaiah 52:7

Notes

Weekly Truth

DAY 21

Scripture is God breathed and true. When we memorize it, we carry the good news of Jesus with us wherever we go.

As we read Acts together, we are memorizing a portion of Peter's sermon in Acts 2. This week, memorize the first part of verse 38.

DATE

[37] When they heard this, they were pierced to the heart and said to Peter and the rest of the apostles, "Brothers, what should we do?" [38] Peter replied, "Repent and be baptized, each of you, in the name of Jesus Christ for the forgiveness of your sins, and you will receive the gift of the Holy Spirit. [39] For the promise is for you and for your children, and for all who are far off, as many as the Lord our God will call."

Acts 2:37–39

SEE TIPS FOR MEMORIZING SCRIPTURE ON PAGE 196.

Acts 14; Jeremiah 2:5; Romans 1:21–23

Mistaken for Gods

ICONIUM, LYSTRA, AND SYRIAN ANTIOCH AD 48

ACTS 14

GROWTH AND PERSECUTION IN ICONIUM

[1] In Iconium they entered the Jewish synagogue, as usual, and spoke in such a way that a great number of both Jews and Greeks believed. [2] But the unbelieving Jews stirred up the Gentiles and poisoned their minds against the brothers. [3] So they stayed there a long time and spoke boldly for the Lord, who testified to the message of his grace by enabling them to do signs and wonders. [4] But the people of the city were divided, some siding with the Jews and others with the apostles. [5] When an attempt was made by both the Gentiles and Jews, with their rulers, to mistreat and stone them, [6] they found out about it and fled to the Lycaonian towns of Lystra and Derbe and to the surrounding countryside. [7] There they continued preaching the gospel.

MISTAKEN FOR GODS IN LYSTRA

[8] In Lystra a man was sitting who was without strength in his feet, had never walked, and had been lame from birth. [9] He listened as Paul spoke. After looking directly at him and seeing that he had faith to be healed,

[10] Paul said in a loud voice, "Stand up on your feet!" And he jumped up and began to walk around.

[11] When the crowds saw what Paul had done, they shouted, saying in the Lycaonian language, "The gods have come down to us in human form!" [12] Barnabas they called Zeus, and Paul, Hermes, because he was the chief speaker. [13] The priest of Zeus, whose temple was just outside the town, brought bulls and wreaths to the gates because he intended, with the crowds, to offer sacrifice.

[14] The apostles Barnabas and Paul tore their robes when they heard this and rushed into the crowd, shouting, [15] "People! Why are you doing these things? We are people also, just like you, and we are proclaiming good news to you, that you turn from these worthless things to the living God, who made the heaven, the earth, the sea, and everything in them. [16] In past generations he allowed all the nations to go their own way, [17] although he did not leave himself without a witness, since he did what is good by giving you rain from heaven and fruitful seasons and filling you with food and your hearts with joy." [18] Even though they said these things, they barely stopped the crowds from sacrificing to them.

[19] Some Jews came from Antioch and Iconium, and when they won over the crowds, they stoned Paul and dragged him out of the city, thinking he was dead. [20] After the disciples gathered around him, he got up and went into the town. The next day he left with Barnabas for Derbe.

CHURCH PLANTING

[21] After they had preached the gospel in that town and made many disciples, they returned to Lystra, to Iconium, and to Antioch, [22] strengthening the disciples by encouraging them to continue in the faith and by telling them, "It is necessary to go through many hardships to enter the kingdom of God." [23] When they had appointed elders for them in every church and prayed with fasting, they committed them to the Lord in whom they had believed.

[24] They passed through Pisidia and came to Pamphylia. [25] After they had spoken the word in Perga, they went down to Attalia. [26] From there they sailed back to Antioch where they had been commended to the grace of God for the work they had now completed. [27] After they arrived and gathered the church together, they reported everything God had done with them and that he had opened the door of faith to the Gentiles. [28] And they spent a considerable time with the disciples.

◖ GOING DEEPER

JEREMIAH 2:5

This is what the LORD says:
What fault did your ancestors find in me
that they went so far from me,
followed worthless idols,
and became worthless themselves?

ROMANS 1:21–23

[21] For though they knew God, they did not glorify him as God or show gratitude. Instead, their thinking became worthless, and their senseless hearts were darkened. [22] Claiming to be wise, they became fools [23] and exchanged the glory of the immortal God for images resembling mortal man, birds, four-footed animals, and reptiles.

Notes

DATE

The Jerusalem Council

DAY 23

Acts 15:1–35; Romans 2:17–24; Galatians 5:1

ACTS 15:1–35

DISPUTE IN ANTIOCH

¹ Some men came down from Judea and began to teach the brothers, "Unless you are circumcised according to the custom prescribed by Moses, you cannot be saved." ² After Paul and Barnabas had engaged them in serious argument and debate, Paul and Barnabas and some others were appointed to go up to the apostles and elders in Jerusalem about this issue. ³ When they had been sent on their way by the church, they passed through both Phoenicia and Samaria, describing in detail the conversion of the Gentiles, and they brought great joy to all the brothers and sisters.

⁴ When they arrived at Jerusalem, they were welcomed by the church, the apostles, and the elders, and they reported all that God had done with them. ⁵ But some of the believers who belonged to the party of the Pharisees stood up and said, "It is necessary to circumcise them and to command them to keep the law of Moses."

THE JERUSALEM COUNCIL

⁶ The apostles and the elders gathered to consider this matter. ⁷ After there had been much debate, Peter stood up and said to them, "Brothers, you are aware that in the early days God made a choice among you, that by my mouth the Gentiles would hear the gospel message and believe. ⁸ And God, who knows the heart, bore witness to them by giving them the Holy Spirit, just as he also did to us. ⁹ He made no distinction between us and them, cleansing their hearts by faith. ¹⁰ Now then, why are you testing God by putting a yoke on the disciples' necks that neither our ancestors nor we have been able to bear? ¹¹ On the contrary, we believe that we are saved through the grace of the Lord Jesus in the same way they are."

¹² The whole assembly became silent and listened to Barnabas and Paul describe all the signs and wonders God had done through them among the Gentiles. ¹³ After they stopped speaking, James responded, "Brothers, listen to me. ¹⁴ Simeon has reported how God first intervened to take from the Gentiles a people for his name. ¹⁵ And the words of the prophets agree with this, as it is written:

¹⁶ After these things I will return
and rebuild David's fallen tent.
I will rebuild its ruins
and set it up again,
¹⁷ so that the rest of humanity
may seek the Lord—
even all the Gentiles
who are called by my name—
declares the Lord
who makes these things ¹⁸ known from long ago.

19 Therefore, in my judgment, we should not cause difficulties for those among the Gentiles who turn to God,

20 but instead we should write to them to abstain from things polluted by idols, from sexual immorality, from eating anything that has been strangled, and from blood. 21 For since ancient times, Moses has had those who proclaim him in every city, and every Sabbath day he is read aloud in the synagogues."

THE LETTER TO THE GENTILE BELIEVERS

22 Then the apostles and the elders, with the whole church, decided to select men who were among them and to send them to Antioch with Paul and Barnabas: Judas, called Barsabbas, and Silas, both leading men among the brothers. 23 They wrote:

"From the apostles and the elders, your brothers,

To the brothers and sisters among the Gentiles in Antioch, Syria, and Cilicia:

Greetings.

24 Since we have heard that some without our authorization went out from us and troubled you with their words and unsettled your hearts, 25 we have unanimously decided to select men and send them to you along with our dearly loved Barnabas and Paul, 26 who have risked their lives for the name of our Lord Jesus Christ. 27 Therefore we have sent Judas and Silas, who will personally report the same things by word of mouth. 28 For it was the Holy Spirit's decision—and ours—not to place further burdens on you beyond these requirements: 29 that you abstain from food offered to idols, from blood, from eating anything that has been strangled, and from sexual immorality. You will do well if you keep yourselves from these things.

Farewell."

THE OUTCOME OF THE JERUSALEM LETTER

30 So they were sent off and went down to Antioch, and after gathering the assembly, they delivered the letter. 31 When they read it, they rejoiced because of its encouragement. 32 Both Judas and Silas, who were also prophets themselves, encouraged the brothers and sisters and strengthened them with a long message. 33 After spending some time there, they were sent back in peace by the brothers and sisters to those who had sent them. 35 But Paul and Barnabas, along with many others, remained in Antioch, teaching and proclaiming the word of the Lord.

● GOING DEEPER

ROMANS 2:17–24

JEWISH VIOLATION OF THE LAW

[17] Now if you call yourself a Jew, and rely on the law, and boast in God, [18] and know his will, and approve the things that are superior, being instructed from the law, [19] and if you are convinced that you are a guide for the blind, a light to those in darkness, [20] an instructor of the ignorant, a teacher of the immature, having the embodiment of knowledge and truth in the law— [21] you then, who teach another, don't you teach yourself? You who preach, "You must not steal"—do you steal? [22] You who say, "You must not commit adultery"—do you commit adultery? You who detest idols, do you rob temples? [23] You who boast in the law, do you dishonor God by breaking the law? [24] For, as it is written: The name of God is blasphemed among the Gentiles because of you.

GALATIANS 5:1

For freedom, Christ set us free. Stand firm, then, and don't submit again to a yoke of slavery.

THE BROTHERS AND SISTERS AT LYSTRA

AND ICONIUM SPOKE HIGHLY OF HIM.

Acts 16:2

Acts 15:36–41; 16:1–15; 1 Corinthians 9:19–21; 1 Timothy 6:11–16

Paul Selects Timothy

ACTS 15:36–41

PAUL AND BARNABAS PART COMPANY

[36] After some time had passed, Paul said to Barnabas, "Let's go back and visit the brothers and sisters in every town where we have preached the word of the Lord and see how they're doing." [37] Barnabas wanted to take along John who was called Mark. [38] But Paul insisted that they should not take along this man who had deserted them in Pamphylia and had not gone on with them to the work. [39] They had such a sharp disagreement that they parted company, and Barnabas took Mark with him and sailed off to Cyprus. [40] But Paul chose Silas and departed, after being commended by the brothers and sisters to the grace of the Lord. [41] He traveled through Syria and Cilicia, strengthening the churches.

ACTS 16:1–15

PAUL SELECTS TIMOTHY

[1] Paul went on to Derbe and Lystra, where there was a disciple named Timothy, the son of a believing Jewish woman, but his father was a Greek. [2] The brothers and sisters at Lystra and Iconium spoke highly of him. [3] Paul wanted Timothy to

DERBE, LYSTRA, GALATIA, TROAS, AND MACEDONIA AD 49–50

go with him; so he took him and circumcised him because of the Jews who were in those places, since they all knew that his father was a Greek. [4] As they traveled through the towns, they delivered the decisions reached by the apostles and elders at Jerusalem for the people to observe. [5] So the churches were strengthened in the faith and grew daily in numbers.

EVANGELIZATION OF EUROPE

[6] They went through the region of Phrygia and Galatia; they had been forbidden by the Holy Spirit to speak the word in Asia. [7] When they came to Mysia, they tried to go into Bithynia, but the Spirit of Jesus did not allow them. [8] Passing by Mysia they went down to Troas. [9] During the night Paul had a vision in which a Macedonian man was standing and pleading with him, "Cross over to Macedonia and help us!" [10] After he had seen the vision, we immediately made efforts to set out for Macedonia, concluding that God had called us to preach the gospel to them.

LYDIA'S CONVERSION

[11] From Troas we put out to sea and sailed straight for Samothrace, the next day to Neapolis, [12] and from there to Philippi, a Roman colony and a leading city of the district of Macedonia. We stayed in that city for several days. [13] On the Sabbath day we went outside the city gate by the river, where we expected to find a place of prayer. We sat down and spoke to the women gathered there. [14] A God-fearing woman named Lydia, a dealer in purple cloth from the city of Thyatira, was listening. The Lord opened her heart to respond to what Paul was saying. [15] After she and her household were baptized, she urged us, "If you consider me a believer in the Lord, come and stay at my house." And she persuaded us.

♥ GOING DEEPER

1 CORINTHIANS 9:19–21

[19] Although I am free from all and not anyone's slave, I have made myself a slave to everyone, in order to win more people. [20] To the Jews I became like a Jew, to win Jews; to those under the law, like one under the law—though I myself am not under the law—to win those under the law. [21] To those who are without the law, like one without the law—though I am not without God's law but under the law of Christ—to win those without the law.

1 TIMOTHY 6:11–16

FIGHT THE GOOD FIGHT

[11] But you, man of God, flee from these things, and pursue righteousness, godliness, faith, love, endurance, and gentleness. [12] Fight the good fight of the faith. Take hold of eternal life to which you were called and about which you have made a good confession in the presence of many witnesses. [13] In the presence of God, who gives life to all, and of Christ Jesus, who gave a good confession before Pontius Pilate, I charge you [14] to keep this command without fault or failure until the appearing of our Lord Jesus Christ. [15] God will bring this about in his own time. He is the blessed and only Sovereign, the King of kings, and the Lord of lords, [16] who alone is immortal and who lives in unapproachable light, whom no one has seen or can see, to him be honor and eternal power. Amen.

Notes

DATE

God the Spirit

The following series of questions and answers from the "God the Spirit" catechism in the *Book of Common Prayer* offers clarity about the person and work of the Holy Spirit.

WHO IS THE HOLY SPIRIT?

The Holy Spirit is the Third Person of the Trinity, God at work in the world and in the Church even now.

JB 32:8; MT 28:19; LK 3:22; JN 14:25–26; 1JN 5:6–8

HOW IS THE HOLY SPIRIT REVEALED IN THE OLD COVENANT?

The Holy Spirit is revealed in the Old Covenant as the giver of life, the One who spoke through the prophets.

GN 1:1–2; JB 33:4; PS 104:30; IS 61:1–3; EZK 2:2; 11:5; JL 2:28

In Acts 2, the Holy Spirit descended on Jewish believers gathered at Pentecost, a fulfillment of God's promise to dwell in His people (Ac 2:17–18). The Spirit's presence throughout the book of Acts equipped and empowered believers to live together as the family of God, to bear spiritual fruit, and to carry the good news of the gospel from Jerusalem to Judea, Samaria, and beyond.

HOW IS THE HOLY SPIRIT REVEALED IN THE NEW COVENANT?

The Holy Spirit is revealed as the Lord who leads us into all truth and enables us to grow in the likeness of Christ.

JN 16:13; AC 1:4–8; 2:16–21; 1CO 2:10–13; 2CO 3:18; 1PT 1:1–2

HOW DO WE RECOGNIZE THE PRESENCE OF THE HOLY SPIRIT IN OUR LIVES?

We recognize the presence of the Holy Spirit when we confess Jesus Christ as Lord and are brought into love and harmony with God, with ourselves, with our neighbors, and with all creation.

PS 139:7; RM 8:1–11; 10:9; EPH 1:13–14; TI 3:6–7; 1JN 4:13–15

HOW DO WE RECOGNIZE THE TRUTHS TAUGHT BY THE HOLY SPIRIT?

We recognize truths to be taught by the Holy Spirit when they are in accord with the Scriptures.

NEH 9:20; PS 143:10; JN 15:26; 1CO 2:10–16; 1TH 1:5; 2TM 3:16–17

Acts 16:16–40; 2 Corinthians 10:3–5; 1 Peter 2:19–21

A Midnight Deliverance

▶ **MACEDONIA
AD 50**

ACTS 16:16–40

PAUL AND SILAS IN PRISON

[16] Once, as we were on our way to prayer, a slave girl met us who had a spirit by which she predicted the future. She made a large profit for her owners by fortune-telling. [17] As she followed Paul and us she cried out, "These men, who are proclaiming to you a way of salvation, are the servants of the Most High God." [18] She did this for many days.

Paul was greatly annoyed. Turning to the spirit, he said, "I command you in the name of Jesus Christ to come out of her!" And it came out right away.

[19] When her owners realized that their hope of profit was gone, they seized Paul and Silas and dragged them into the marketplace to the authorities. [20] Bringing them before the chief magistrates, they said, "These men are seriously disturbing our city. They are Jews [21] and are promoting customs that are not legal for us as Romans to adopt or practice." [22] The crowd joined in the attack against them, and the chief magistrates stripped off their clothes and ordered them to be beaten with rods. [23] After they had severely flogged them, they threw them in jail, ordering the jailer to guard them carefully. [24] Receiving such an order, he put them into the inner prison and secured their feet in the stocks.

²⁵ About midnight Paul and Silas were praying and singing hymns to God, and the prisoners were listening to them. ²⁶ Suddenly there was such a violent earthquake that the foundations of the jail were shaken, and immediately all the doors were opened, and everyone's chains came loose. ²⁷ When the jailer woke up and saw the doors of the prison standing open, he drew his sword and was going to kill himself, since he thought the prisoners had escaped.

²⁸ But Paul called out in a loud voice, "Don't harm yourself, because we're all here!"

²⁹ The jailer called for lights, rushed in, and fell down trembling before Paul and Silas. ³⁰ He escorted them out and said, "Sirs, what must I do to be saved?"

³¹ They said, "Believe in the Lord Jesus, and you will be saved—you and your household."

³² And they spoke the word of the Lord to him along with everyone in his house. ³³ He took them the same hour of the night and washed their wounds. Right away he and all his family were baptized. ³⁴ He brought them into his house, set a meal before them, and rejoiced because he had come to believe in God with his entire household.

AN OFFICIAL APOLOGY

³⁵ When daylight came, the chief magistrates sent the police to say, "Release those men."

³⁶ The jailer reported these words to Paul: "The magistrates have sent orders for you to be released. So come out now and go in peace."

³⁷ But Paul said to them, "They beat us in public without a trial, although we are Roman citizens, and threw us in jail. And now are they going to send us away secretly? Certainly not! On the contrary, let them come themselves and escort us out."

³⁸ The police reported these words to the magistrates. They were afraid when they heard that Paul and Silas were Roman citizens. ³⁹ So they came to appease them, and escorting them from prison, they urged them to leave town. ⁴⁰ After leaving the jail, they came to Lydia's house, where they saw and encouraged the brothers and sisters, and departed.

◆ GOING DEEPER

2 CORINTHIANS 10:3–5

³ For although we live in the flesh, we do not wage war according to the flesh, ⁴ since the weapons of our warfare are not of the flesh, but are powerful through God for the demolition of strongholds. We demolish arguments ⁵ and every proud thing that is raised up against the knowledge of God, and we take every thought captive to obey Christ.

1 PETER 2:19–21

¹⁹ For it brings favor if, because of a consciousness of God, someone endures grief from suffering unjustly. ²⁰ For what credit is there if when you do wrong and are beaten, you endure it? But when you do what is good and suffer, if you endure it, this brings favor with God.

²¹ For you were called to this, because Christ also suffered for you, leaving you an example, that you should follow in his steps.

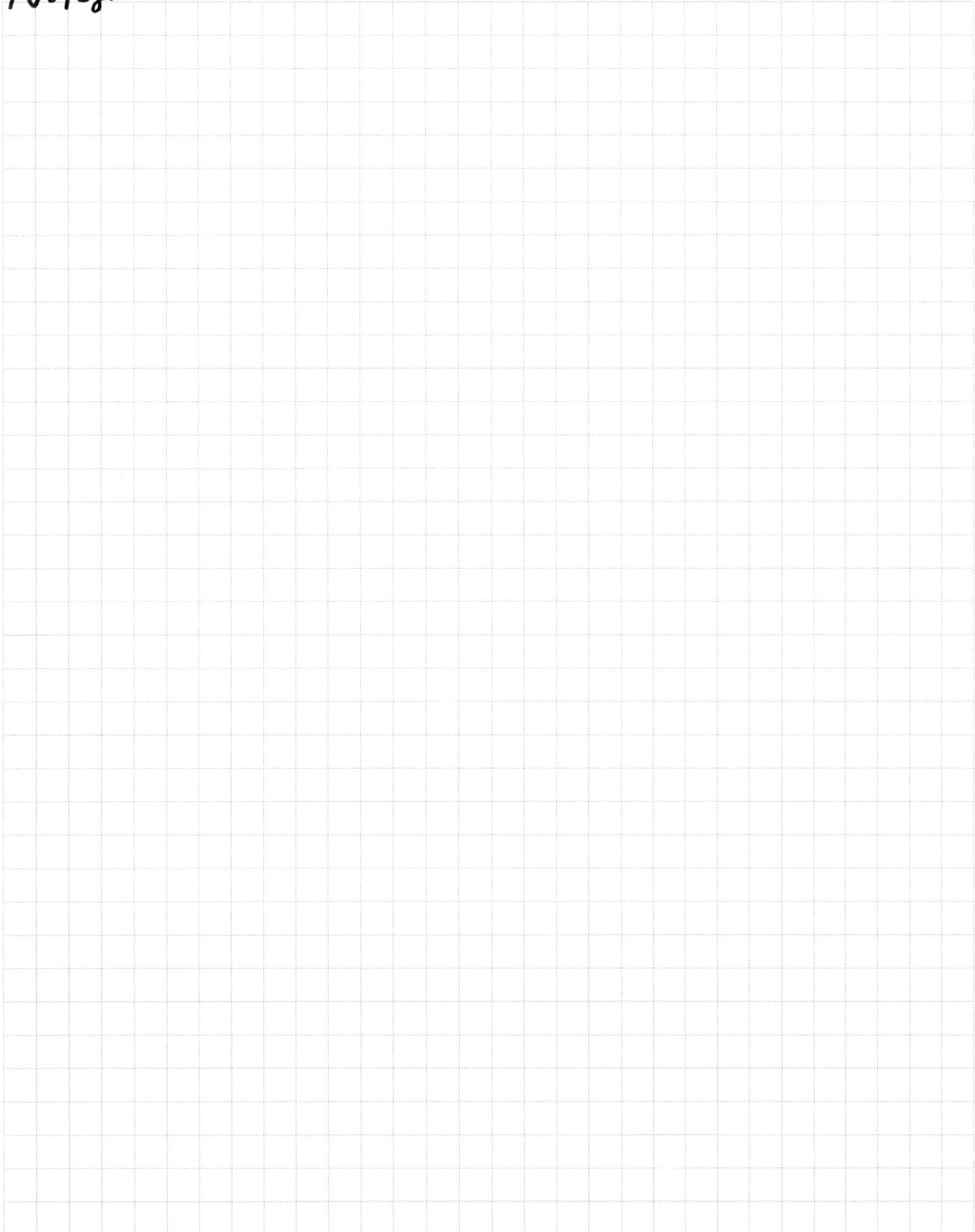

Notes

DATE

THE GOD WHO MADE THE WORLD AND EVERYTHING IN IT—HE

IS LORD OF HEAVEN AND EARTH—DOES NOT LIVE IN SHRINES

MADE BY HANDS. NEITHER IS HE SERVED BY HUMAN HANDS,

AS THOUGH HE NEEDED ANYTHING, SINCE HE HIMSELF GIVES

EVERYONE LIFE AND BREATH AND ALL THINGS.

Acts 17:24–25

Acts 17; Isaiah 42:8; Romans 3:21–26

Paul Preaches at the Areopagus

ACTS 17

A SHORT MINISTRY IN THESSALONICA

THESSALONICA, BEREA, AND ATHENS
AD 50

¹ After they passed through Amphipolis and Apollonia, they came to Thessalonica, where there was a Jewish synagogue. ² As usual, Paul went into the synagogue, and on three Sabbath days reasoned with them from the Scriptures, ³ explaining and proving that it was necessary for the Messiah to suffer and rise from the dead: "This Jesus I am proclaiming to you is the Messiah." ⁴ Some of them were persuaded and joined Paul and Silas, including a large number of God-fearing Greeks, as well as a number of the leading women.

RIOT IN THE CITY

⁵ But the Jews became jealous, and they brought together some wicked men from the marketplace, formed a mob, and started a riot in the city. Attacking Jason's house, they searched for them to bring them out to the public assembly. ⁶ When they did not find them, they dragged Jason and some of the brothers before the city officials, shouting, "These men who have turned the world upside down have come here too, ⁷ and Jason has welcomed them. They are all acting contrary to Caesar's decrees, saying that there is another king—Jesus." ⁸ The crowd and city officials who heard these things were upset. ⁹ After taking a security bond from Jason and the others, they released them.

[10] As soon as it was night, the brothers and sisters sent Paul and Silas away to Berea. Upon arrival, they went into the synagogue of the Jews. [11] The people here were of more noble character than those in Thessalonica, since they received the word with eagerness and examined the Scriptures daily to see if these things were so. [12] Consequently, many of them believed, including a number of the prominent Greek women as well as men. [13] But when the Jews from Thessalonica found out that the word of God had been proclaimed by Paul at Berea, they came there too, agitating and upsetting the crowds. [14] Then the brothers and sisters immediately sent Paul away to go to the coast, but Silas and Timothy stayed on there. [15] Those who escorted Paul brought him as far as Athens, and after receiving instructions for Silas and Timothy to come to him as quickly as possible, they departed.

PAUL IN ATHENS

[16] While Paul was waiting for them in Athens, he was deeply distressed when he saw that the city was full of idols. [17] So he reasoned in the synagogue with the Jews and with those who worshiped God, as well as in the marketplace every day with those who happened to be there. [18] Some of the Epicurean and Stoic philosophers also debated with him. Some said, "What is this ignorant show-off trying to say?"

Others replied, "He seems to be a preacher of foreign deities"—because he was telling the good news about Jesus and the resurrection.

[19] They took him and brought him to the Areopagus, and said, "May we learn about this new teaching you are presenting? [20] Because what you say sounds strange to us, and we want to know what these things mean." [21] Now all the Athenians and the foreigners residing there spent their time on nothing else but telling or hearing something new.

THE AREOPAGUS ADDRESS

[22] Paul stood in the middle of the Areopagus and said, "People of Athens! I see that you are extremely religious in every respect. [23] For as I was passing through and observing the objects of your worship, I even found an altar on which was inscribed, 'To an Unknown God.' Therefore, what you worship in ignorance, this I proclaim to you. [24] The God who made the world and everything in it—he is Lord of heaven and earth—does not live in shrines made by hands. [25] Neither is he served by human hands, as though he needed anything, since he himself gives everyone life and breath and all things. [26] From one man he has made every nationality to live over the whole earth and has determined their appointed times and the boundaries of where they live.

[27] **He did this so that they might seek God, and perhaps they might reach out and find him, though he is not far from each one of us.**

[28] For in him we live and move and have our being, as even some of your own poets have said, 'For we are also his offspring.' [29] Since, then, we are God's offspring, we shouldn't think that the divine nature is like gold or silver or stone, an image fashioned by human art and imagination.

[30] "Therefore, having overlooked the times of ignorance, God now commands all people everywhere to repent, [31] because he has set a day when he is going to judge the world in righteousness by the man he has appointed. He has provided proof of this to everyone by raising him from the dead."

[32] When they heard about the resurrection of the dead, some began to ridicule him, but others said, "We'd like to hear from you again about this." [33] So Paul left their presence. [34] However, some people joined him and believed, including Dionysius the Areopagite, a woman named Damaris, and others with them.

◆ GOING DEEPER

ISAIAH 42:8

"I am the LORD. That is my name,
and I will not give my glory to another
or my praise to idols."

ROMANS 3:21–26

THE RIGHTEOUSNESS OF GOD THROUGH FAITH

[21] But now, apart from the law, the righteousness of God has been revealed, attested by the Law and the Prophets. [22] The righteousness of God is through faith in Jesus Christ to all who believe, since there is no distinction. [23] For all have sinned and fall short of the glory of God; [24] they are justified freely by his grace through the redemption that is in Christ Jesus. [25] God presented him as the mercy seat by his blood, through faith, to demonstrate his righteousness, because in his restraint God passed over the sins previously committed. [26] God presented him to demonstrate his righteousness at the present time, so that he would be just and justify the one who has faith in Jesus.

Notes

Week 4 Reflection

> Look over the key themes you marked in this week's readings. What did you notice about the Holy Spirit, the early Church, and the spread of the gospel?

How do you see these themes at work in your life, community, and local church today?

Grace Day

Take this day to catch up on your reading,
pray, and rest in the presence of the Lord.

FOR FREEDOM, CHRIST SET US FREE. STAND FIRM, THEN,

AND DON'T SUBMIT AGAIN TO A YOKE OF SLAVERY.

Galatians 5:1

Notes

Weekly Truth

Scripture is God breathed and true. When we memorize it, we carry the good news of Jesus with us wherever we go.

As we read Acts together, we are memorizing a portion of Peter's sermon in Acts 2. This week, memorize all of verse 38.

DATE

[37] When they heard this, they were pierced to the heart and said to Peter and the rest of the apostles, "Brothers, what should we do?" [38] Peter replied, "Repent and be baptized, each of you, in the name of Jesus Christ for the forgiveness of your sins, and you will receive the gift of the Holy Spirit. [39] For the promise is for you and for your children, and for all who are far off, as many as the Lord our God will call."

Acts 2:37–39

SEE TIPS FOR MEMORIZING SCRIPTURE ON PAGE 196.

The Lord said to Paul in
a night vision, "Don't be
afraid, but keep on speaking
and don't be silent."

ACTS 18:9

Acts 18; Matthew 10:26–31; 1 Corinthians 1:1–9

Founding the Corinthian Church

ACTS 18

FOUNDING THE CORINTHIAN CHURCH

[1] After this, he left Athens and went to Corinth, [2] where he found a Jew named Aquila, a native of Pontus, who had recently come from Italy with his wife Priscilla because Claudius had ordered all the Jews to leave Rome. Paul came to them, [3] and since they were of the same occupation, tentmakers by trade, he stayed with them and worked. [4] He reasoned in the synagogue every Sabbath and tried to persuade both Jews and Greeks.

[5] When Silas and Timothy arrived from Macedonia, Paul devoted himself to preaching the word and testified to the Jews that Jesus is the Messiah. [6] When they resisted and blasphemed, he shook out his clothes and told them, "Your blood is on your own heads! I am innocent. From now on I will go to the Gentiles." [7] So he left there and went to the house of a man named Titius Justus, a worshiper of God, whose house was next door to the synagogue. [8] Crispus, the leader of the synagogue, believed in the Lord, along with his whole household. Many of the Corinthians, when they heard, believed and were baptized.

[9] The Lord said to Paul in a night vision, "Don't be afraid, but keep on speaking and don't be silent. [10] For I am with you, and no one will lay a hand on you to hurt you, because I have many people in this city." [11] He stayed there a year and a half, teaching the word of God among them.

> CORINTH, EPHESUS, JERUSALEM, AND SYRIAN ANTIOCH AD 50–52

¹² While Gallio was proconsul of Achaia, the Jews made a united attack against Paul and brought him to the tribunal. ¹³ "This man," they said, "is persuading people to worship God in ways contrary to the law."

¹⁴ As Paul was about to open his mouth, Gallio said to the Jews, "If it were a matter of wrongdoing or of a serious crime, it would be reasonable for me to put up with you Jews. ¹⁵ But if these are questions about words, names, and your own law, see to it yourselves. I refuse to be a judge of such things." ¹⁶ So he drove them from the tribunal. ¹⁷ And they all seized Sosthenes, the leader of the synagogue, and beat him in front of the tribunal, but none of these things mattered to Gallio.

THE RETURN TRIP TO ANTIOCH

¹⁸ After staying for some time, Paul said farewell to the brothers and sisters and sailed away to Syria, accompanied by Priscilla and Aquila. He shaved his head at Cenchreae because of a vow he had taken. ¹⁹ When they reached Ephesus he left them there, but he himself entered the synagogue and debated with the Jews. ²⁰ When they asked him to stay for a longer time, he declined, ²¹ but he said farewell and added, "I'll come back to you again, if God wills." Then he set sail from Ephesus.

²² On landing at Caesarea, he went up to Jerusalem and greeted the church, then went down to Antioch.

²³ After spending some time there, he set out, traveling through one place after another in the region of Galatia and Phrygia, strengthening all the disciples.

THE ELOQUENT APOLLOS

²⁴ Now a Jew named Apollos, a native Alexandrian, an eloquent man who was competent in the use of the Scriptures, arrived in Ephesus. ²⁵ He had been instructed in the way of the Lord; and being fervent in spirit, he was speaking and teaching accurately about Jesus, although he knew only John's baptism. ²⁶ He began to speak boldly in the synagogue. After Priscilla and Aquila heard him, they took him aside and explained the way of God to him more accurately. ²⁷ When he wanted to cross over to Achaia, the brothers and sisters wrote to the disciples to welcome him. After he arrived, he was a great help to those who by grace had believed. ²⁸ For he vigorously refuted the Jews in public, demonstrating through the Scriptures that Jesus is the Messiah.

❤ GOING DEEPER

MATTHEW 10:26–31
FEAR GOD

²⁶ "Therefore, don't be afraid of them, since there is nothing covered that won't be uncovered and nothing hidden that won't be made known. ²⁷ What I tell you in the dark, speak in the light. What you hear in a whisper, proclaim on the housetops. ²⁸ Don't fear those who kill the body but are not able to kill the soul; rather, fear him who is able to destroy both soul and body in hell. ²⁹ Aren't two sparrows sold for a penny? Yet not one of them falls to the ground without your Father's consent. ³⁰ But even the hairs of your head have all been counted. ³¹ So don't be afraid; you are worth more than many sparrows."

1 CORINTHIANS 1:1–9
GREETING

¹ Paul, called as an apostle of Christ Jesus by God's will, and Sosthenes our brother:

² To the church of God at Corinth, to those sanctified in Christ Jesus, called as saints, with all those in every place who call on the name of Jesus Christ our Lord—both their Lord and ours.

³ Grace to you and peace from God our Father and the Lord Jesus Christ.

THANKSGIVING

⁴ I always thank my God for you because of the grace of God given to you in Christ Jesus, ⁵ that you were enriched in him in every way, in all speech and all knowledge. ⁶ In this way, the testimony about Christ was confirmed among you, ⁷ so that you do not lack any spiritual gift as you eagerly wait for the revelation of our Lord Jesus Christ. ⁸ He will also strengthen you to the end, so that you will be blameless in the day of our Lord Jesus Christ. ⁹ God is faithful; you were called by him into fellowship with his Son, Jesus Christ our Lord.

Notes

DATE

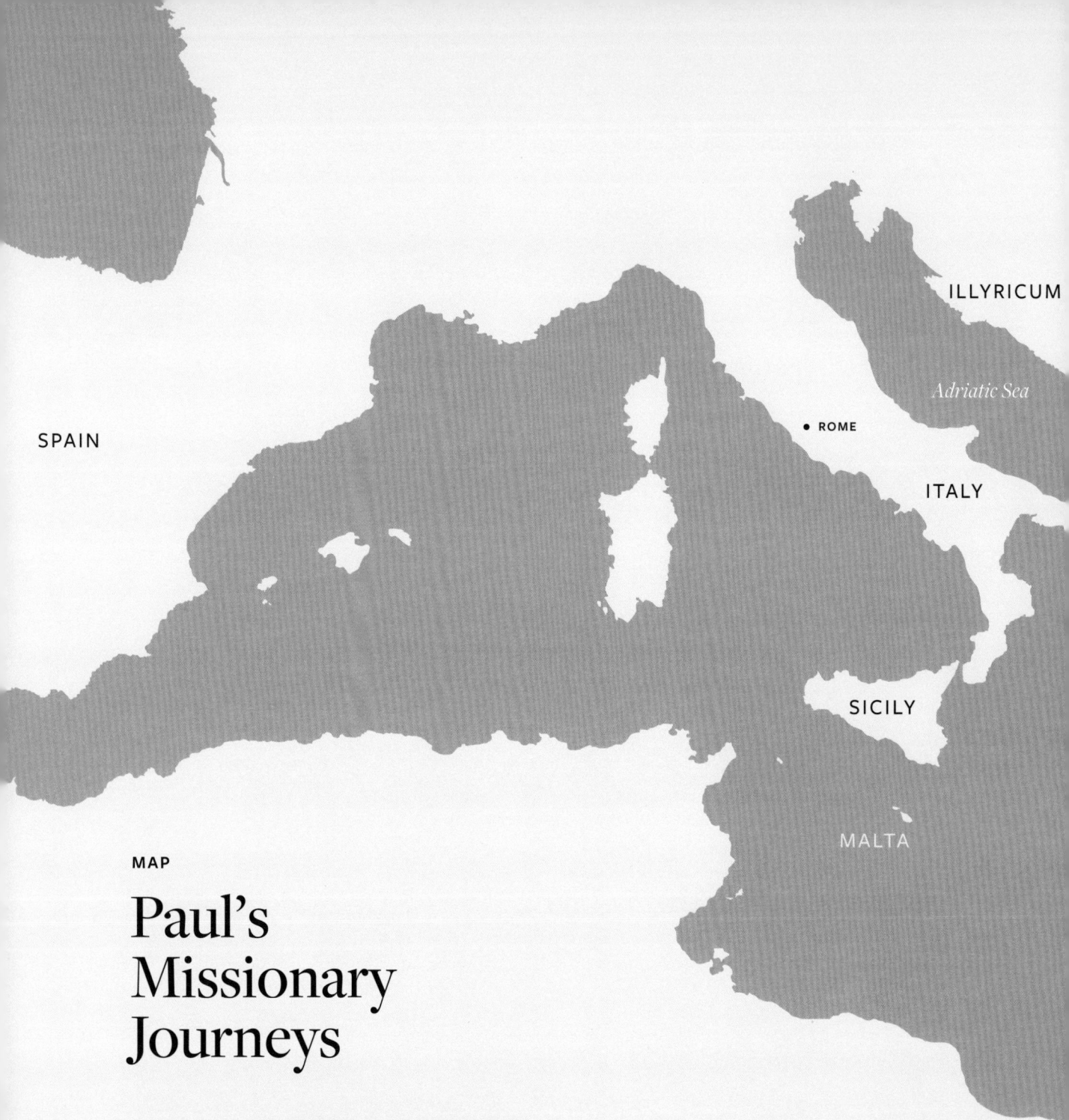

ILLYRICUM

Adriatic Sea

SPAIN

• ROME

ITALY

SICILY

MALTA

Paul's Missionary Journeys

In Acts 1:8, Jesus told His apostles to share the gospel with people "in Jerusalem, in all Judea and Samaria, and to the ends of the earth." His followers began to carry out His instructions after Pentecost (Ac 2). Paul and his fellow coworkers in the gospel were the first to undertake the mission of traveling and sharing the gospel—establishing churches throughout the region and encouraging others as their numbers grew (Ac 18:19–21). This map highlights these locations, as well as the other places Paul visited on his missionary journeys.

N

0 MI	100	200	300

0 KM	100	200	300	400

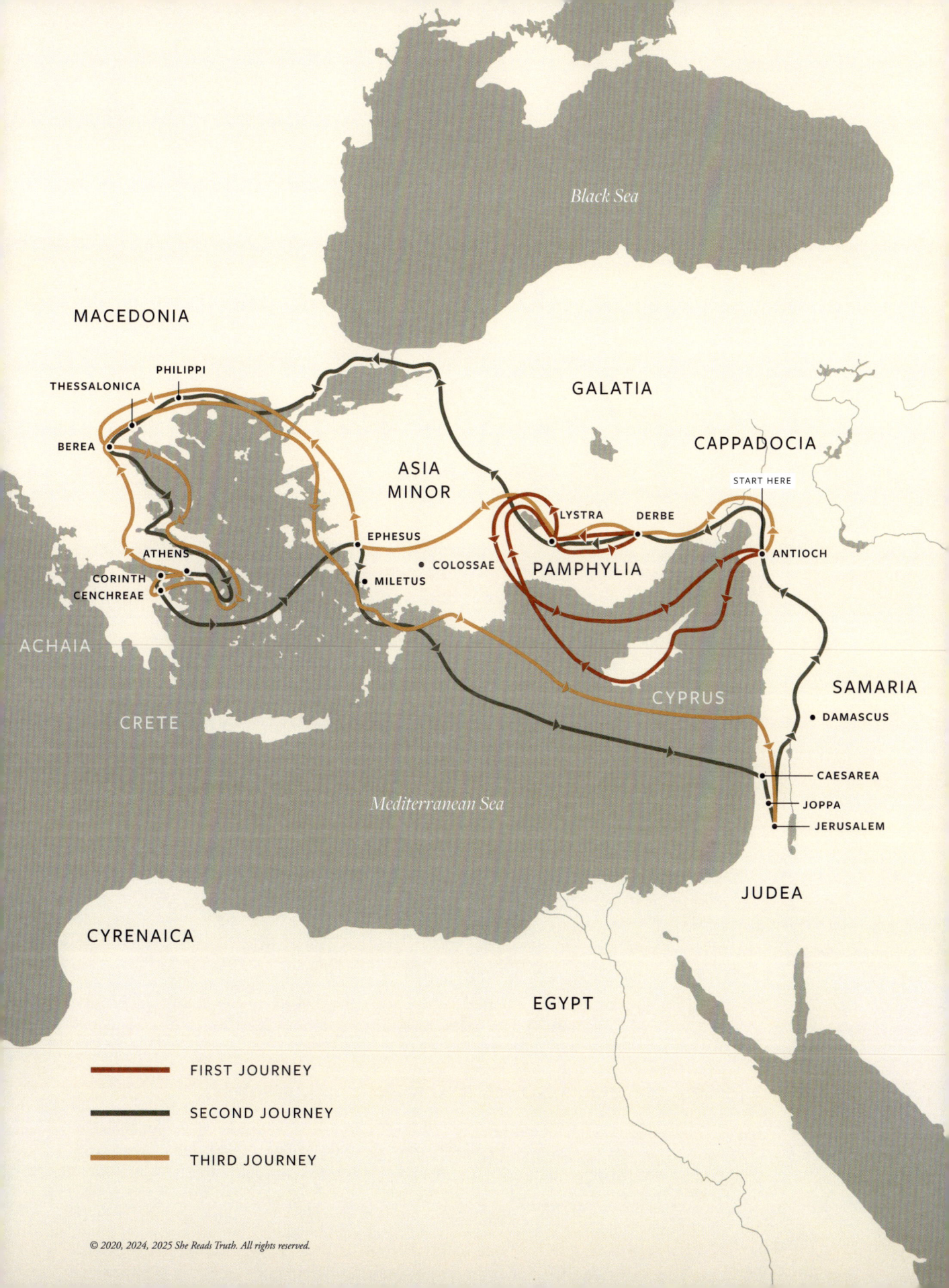

Black Sea

MACEDONIA

GALATIA

CAPPADOCIA

THESSALONICA

PHILIPPI

BEREA

ASIA
MINOR

START HERE

LYSTRA   DERBE

ATHENS

EPHESUS

COLOSSAE

ANTIOCH

CORINTH

MILETUS

PAMPHYLIA

CENCHREAE

ACHAIA

CYPRUS

SAMARIA

CRETE

DAMASCUS

CAESAREA

Mediterranean Sea

JOPPA

JERUSALEM

CYRENAICA

JUDEA

EGYPT

FIRST JOURNEY

SECOND JOURNEY

THIRD JOURNEY

Acts 19; Isaiah 44:9–11; Ephesians 6:12

The Gospel in Ephesus

▶ **EPHESUS**
AD 53–55

ACTS 19

TWELVE DISCIPLES OF JOHN THE BAPTIST

[1] While Apollos was in Corinth, Paul traveled through the interior regions and came to Ephesus. He found some disciples [2] and asked them, "Did you receive the Holy Spirit when you believed?"

"No," they told him, "we haven't even heard that there is a Holy Spirit."

[3] "Into what then were you baptized?" he asked them.

"Into John's baptism," they replied.

[4] Paul said, "John baptized with a baptism of repentance, telling the people that they should believe in the one who would come after him, that is, in Jesus."

[5] When they heard this, they were baptized into the name of the Lord Jesus. [6] And when Paul had laid his hands on them, the Holy Spirit came on them, and they began to speak in tongues and to prophesy. [7] Now there were about twelve men in all.

IN THE LECTURE HALL OF TYRANNUS

[8] Paul entered the synagogue and spoke boldly over a period of three months, arguing and persuading them about the kingdom of God. [9] But when some

became hardened and would not believe, slandering the Way in front of the crowd, he withdrew from them, taking the disciples, and conducted discussions every day in the lecture hall of Tyrannus. [10] This went on for two years, so that all the residents of Asia, both Jews and Greeks, heard the word of the Lord.

DEMONISM DEFEATED AT EPHESUS

[11] God was performing extraordinary miracles by Paul's hands, [12] so that even facecloths or aprons that had touched his skin were brought to the sick, and the diseases left them, and the evil spirits came out of them.

[13] Now some of the itinerant Jewish exorcists also attempted to pronounce the name of the Lord Jesus over those who had evil spirits, saying, "I command you by the Jesus that Paul preaches!" [14] Seven sons of Sceva, a Jewish high priest, were doing this. [15] The evil spirit answered them, "I know Jesus, and I recognize Paul—but who are you?" [16] Then the man who had the evil spirit jumped on them, overpowered them all, and prevailed against them, so that they ran out of that house naked and wounded.

[17] **When this became known to everyone who lived in Ephesus, both Jews and Greeks, they became afraid, and the name of the Lord Jesus was held in high esteem.**

[18] And many who had become believers came confessing and disclosing their practices, [19] while many of those who had practiced magic collected their books and burned them in front of everyone. So they calculated their value and found it to be fifty thousand pieces of silver. [20] In this way the word of the Lord spread and prevailed.

THE RIOT IN EPHESUS

[21] After these events, Paul resolved by the Spirit to pass through Macedonia and Achaia and go to Jerusalem. "After I've been there," he said, "It is necessary for me to see Rome as well." [22] After sending to Macedonia two of those who assisted him, Timothy and Erastus, he himself stayed in Asia for a while.

[23] About that time there was a major disturbance about the Way. [24] For a person named Demetrius, a silversmith who made silver shrines of Artemis, provided a great deal of business for the craftsmen. [25] When he had assembled them, as well as the workers engaged in this type of business, he said, "Men, you know that our prosperity is derived from this business. [26] You see and hear that not only in Ephesus, but in almost all of Asia, this man Paul has persuaded and misled a considerable number of people by saying that gods made by hand are not gods. [27] Not only do we run a risk that our business may be discredited, but also that the temple of the great goddess Artemis may be despised and her magnificence come to the verge of ruin—the very one all of Asia and the world worship."

[28] When they had heard this, they were filled with rage and began to cry out, "Great is Artemis of the Ephesians!" [29] So the city was filled with confusion, and they rushed all together into the amphitheater, dragging along Gaius and Aristarchus, Macedonians who were Paul's traveling companions. [30] Although Paul wanted to go in before the people, the disciples did not let him. [31] Even some of the provincial officials of Asia, who were his friends, sent word to him, pleading with him not to venture into the amphitheater. [32] Some were shouting one thing and some another, because the assembly was in confusion, and most of them did not know why they had come together. [33] Some Jews in the crowd gave instructions to Alexander after they pushed him to the front. Motioning with his hand, Alexander wanted to make his defense to the people. [34] But when they recognized that he was a Jew, they all shouted in unison for about two hours, "Great is Artemis of the Ephesians!"

[35] When the city clerk had calmed the crowd down, he said, "People of Ephesus! What person is there who doesn't know that the city of the Ephesians is the temple guardian of the great Artemis, and of the image that fell from heaven? [36] Therefore, since these things are undeniable, you must keep calm and not do anything rash. [37] For you have brought these men here who are not temple robbers or blasphemers of our goddess. [38] So if Demetrius and the craftsmen who are with him have a case against anyone, the courts are in

session, and there are proconsuls. Let them bring charges against one another. [39] But if you seek anything further, it must be decided in a legal assembly. [40] In fact, we run a risk of being charged with rioting for what happened today, since there is no justification that we can give as a reason for this disturbance." [41] After saying this, he dismissed the assembly.

Notes

GOING DEEPER

ISAIAH 44:9–11

[9] All who make idols are nothing,
and what they treasure benefits no one.
Their witnesses do not see or know anything,
so they will be put to shame.
[10] Who makes a god or casts a metal image
that benefits no one?
[11] Look, all its worshipers will be put to shame,
and the craftsmen are humans.
They all will assemble and stand;
they all will be startled and put to shame.

EPHESIANS 6:12

For our struggle is not against flesh and blood, but against the rulers, against the authorities, against the cosmic powers of this darkness, against evil, spiritual forces in the heavens.

I DID NOT AVOID DECLARING TO YOU THE WHOLE PLAN OF GOD.

Acts 20:27

Acts 20; 2 Corinthians 5:18–20; Romans 15:18–19

Paul's Farewell Address to the Ephesians

ACTS 20

PAUL IN MACEDONIA

[1] After the uproar was over, Paul sent for the disciples, encouraged them, and after saying farewell, departed to go to Macedonia. [2] And when he had passed through those areas and offered them many words of encouragement, he came to Greece [3] and stayed three months. The Jews plotted against him when he was about to set sail for Syria, and so he decided to go back through Macedonia. [4] He was accompanied by Sopater son of Pyrrhus from Berea, Aristarchus and Secundus from Thessalonica, Gaius from Derbe, Timothy, and Tychicus and Trophimus from the province of Asia. [5] These men went on ahead and waited for us in Troas, [6] but we sailed away from Philippi after the Festival of Unleavened Bread. In five days we reached them at Troas, where we spent seven days.

EUTYCHUS REVIVED AT TROAS

[7] On the first day of the week, we assembled to break bread. Paul spoke to them, and since he was about to depart the next day, he kept on talking until midnight. [8] There were many lamps in the room upstairs where we were assembled, [9] and a young man named Eutychus was sitting on a window sill and sank into a deep sleep as Paul kept on talking. When he was overcome by sleep, he fell down from

TROAS AND MILETUS AD 56–57

the third story and was picked up dead. [10] But Paul went down, bent over him, embraced him, and said, "Don't be alarmed, because he's alive." [11] After going upstairs, breaking the bread, and eating, Paul talked a long time until dawn. Then he left. [12] They brought the boy home alive and were greatly comforted.

FROM TROAS TO MILETUS

[13] We went on ahead to the ship and sailed for Assos, where we were going to take Paul on board, because these were his instructions, since he himself was going by land. [14] When he met us at Assos, we took him on board and went on to Mitylene. [15] Sailing from there, the next day we arrived off Chios. The following day we crossed over to Samos, and the day after, we came to Miletus. [16] For Paul had decided to sail past Ephesus to avoid spending time in the province of Asia, because he was hurrying to be in Jerusalem, if possible, for the day of Pentecost.

FAREWELL ADDRESS TO THE EPHESIAN ELDERS

[17] Now from Miletus, he sent to Ephesus and summoned the elders of the church. [18] When they came to him, he said to them, "You know, from the first day I set foot in Asia, how I was with you the whole time, [19] serving the Lord with all humility, with tears, and during the trials that came to me through the plots of the Jews. [20] You know that I did not avoid proclaiming to you anything that was profitable or from teaching you publicly and from house to house. [21] I testified to both Jews and Greeks about repentance toward God and faith in our Lord Jesus.

[22] "And now I am on my way to Jerusalem, compelled by the Spirit, not knowing what I will encounter there, [23] except that in every town the Holy Spirit warns me that chains and afflictions are waiting for me. [24] But I consider my life of no value to myself; my purpose is to finish my course and the ministry I received from the Lord Jesus, to testify to the gospel of God's grace.

[25] "And now I know that none of you, among whom I went about preaching the kingdom, will ever see me again. [26] Therefore I declare to you this day that I am innocent of the blood of all of you, [27] because I did not avoid declaring to you the whole plan of God.

[28] Be on guard for yourselves and for all the flock of which the Holy Spirit has appointed you as overseers, to shepherd the church of God, which he purchased with his own blood.

[29] I know that after my departure savage wolves will come in among you, not sparing the flock. [30] Men will rise up even from your own number and distort the truth to lure the disciples into following them. [31] Therefore be on the alert, remembering that night and day for three years I never stopped warning each one of you with tears.

[32] "And now I commit you to God and to the word of his grace, which is able to build you up and to give you an inheritance among all who are sanctified. [33] I have not coveted anyone's silver or gold or clothing. [34] You yourselves know that I worked with my own hands to support myself and those who are with me. [35] In every way I've shown you that it is necessary to help the weak by laboring like this and to remember the words of the Lord Jesus, because he said, 'It is more blessed to give than to receive.'"

[36] After he said this, he knelt down and prayed with all of them. [37] There were many tears shed by everyone. They embraced Paul and kissed him, [38] grieving most of all over his statement that they would never see his face again. And they accompanied him to the ship.

◆ GOING DEEPER

2 CORINTHIANS 5:18–20

[18] Everything is from God, who has reconciled us to himself through Christ and has given us the ministry of reconciliation. [19] That is, in Christ, God was reconciling the world to himself, not counting their trespasses against them, and he has committed the message of reconciliation to us.

[20] Therefore, we are ambassadors for Christ, since God is making his appeal through us. We plead on Christ's behalf, "Be reconciled to God."

ROMANS 15:18–19

[18] For I would not dare say anything except what Christ has accomplished through me by word and deed for the obedience of the Gentiles, [19] by the power of miraculous signs and wonders, and by the power of God's Spirit. As a result, I have fully proclaimed the gospel of Christ from Jerusalem all the way around to Illyricum.

Acts 21:1–36; Matthew 5:11–12; Philippians 1:20–21

Paul's Determination to Reach Jerusalem

CAESAREA MARITIMA AND JERUSALEM AD 57

ACTS 21:1–36

WARNINGS ON THE JOURNEY TO JERUSALEM

[1] After we tore ourselves away from them, we set sail straight for Cos, the next day to Rhodes, and from there to Patara. [2] Finding a ship crossing over to Phoenicia, we boarded and set sail. [3] After we sighted Cyprus, passing to the south of it, we sailed on to Syria and arrived at Tyre, since the ship was to unload its cargo there. [4] We sought out the disciples and stayed there seven days. Through the Spirit they told Paul not to go to Jerusalem. [5] When our time had come to an end, we left to continue our journey, while all of them, with their wives and children, accompanied us out of the city. After kneeling down on the beach to pray, [6] we said farewell to one another and boarded the ship, and they returned home.

[7] When we completed our voyage from Tyre, we reached Ptolemais, where we greeted the brothers and sisters and stayed with them for a day. [8] The next day we left and came to Caesarea, where we entered the house of Philip the evangelist, who was one of the Seven, and stayed with him. [9] This man had four virgin daughters who prophesied.

[10] After we had been there for several days, a prophet named Agabus came down from Judea. [11] He came to us, took Paul's belt, tied his own feet and hands, and said, "This is what the Holy Spirit says: 'In this way the Jews in Jerusalem will bind the man who owns this belt and deliver him over to the Gentiles.'" [12] When we heard this, both we and the local people pleaded with him not to go up to Jerusalem.

WEEK 5

[13] Then Paul replied, "What are you doing, weeping and breaking my heart? For I am ready not only to be bound but also to die in Jerusalem for the name of the Lord Jesus."

[14] Since he would not be persuaded, we said no more except, "The Lord's will be done."

CONFLICT OVER THE GENTILE MISSION

[15] After this we got ready and went up to Jerusalem. [16] Some of the disciples from Caesarea also went with us and brought us to Mnason of Cyprus, an early disciple, with whom we were to stay.

[17] When we reached Jerusalem, the brothers and sisters welcomed us warmly. [18] The following day Paul went in with us to James, and all the elders were present. [19] After greeting them, he reported in detail what God had done among the Gentiles through his ministry.

[20] When they heard it, they glorified God and said, "You see, brother, how many thousands of Jews there are who have believed, and they are all zealous for the law. [21] But they have been informed about you—that you are teaching all the Jews who are among the Gentiles to abandon Moses, telling them not to circumcise their children or to live according to our customs. [22] So what is to be done? They will certainly hear that you've come. [23] Therefore do what we tell you: We have four men who have made a vow. [24] Take these men, purify yourself along with them, and pay for them to get their heads shaved. Then everyone will know that what they were told about you amounts to nothing, but that you yourself are also careful about observing the law. [25] With regard to the Gentiles who have believed, we have written a letter containing our decision that they should keep themselves from food sacrificed to idols, from blood, from what is strangled, and from sexual immorality."

THE RIOT IN THE TEMPLE

[26] So the next day, Paul took the men, having purified himself along with them, and entered the temple, announcing the completion of the purification days when the offering would be made for each of them. [27] When the seven days were nearly over, some Jews from the province of Asia saw him in the temple, stirred up the whole crowd, and seized him, [28] shouting, "Fellow Israelites, help! This is the man who teaches everyone everywhere against our people, our law, and this place. What's more, he also brought Greeks into the temple and has defiled this holy place." [29] For they had previously seen Trophimus the Ephesian in the city with him, and they supposed that Paul had brought him into the temple.

[30] The whole city was stirred up, and the people rushed together. They seized Paul, dragged him out of the temple, and at once the gates were shut.

Notes

[31] As they were trying to kill him, word went up to the commander of the regiment that all Jerusalem was in chaos. [32] Taking along soldiers and centurions, he immediately ran down to them. Seeing the commander and the soldiers, they stopped beating Paul. [33] Then the commander approached, took him into custody, and ordered him to be bound with two chains. He asked who he was and what he had done. [34] Some in the crowd were shouting one thing and some another. Since he was not able to get reliable information because of the uproar, he ordered him to be taken into the barracks. [35] When Paul got to the steps, he had to be carried by the soldiers because of the violence of the crowd, [36] for the mass of people followed, yelling, "Get rid of him!"

◖ GOING DEEPER

MATTHEW 5:11-12

[11] "You are blessed when they insult you and persecute you and falsely say every kind of evil against you because of me. [12] Be glad and rejoice, because your reward is great in heaven. For that is how they persecuted the prophets who were before you."

PHILIPPIANS 1:20-21

[20] My eager expectation and hope is that I will not be ashamed about anything, but that now as always, with all courage, Christ will be highly honored in my body, whether by life or by death.

LIVING IS CHRIST

[21] For me, to live is Christ and to die is gain.

Notes

DATE

Paul Before the Sanhedrin

DAY 33

Acts 21:37–40; 22; 23:1–11; Hebrews 10:19–22

ACTS 21:37-40

PAUL'S DEFENSE BEFORE THE JERUSALEM MOB

³⁷ As he was about to be brought into the barracks, Paul said to the commander, "Am I allowed to say something to you?"

He replied, "You know how to speak Greek? ³⁸ Aren't you the Egyptian who started a revolt some time ago and led four thousand men of the Assassins into the wilderness?"

³⁹ Paul said, "I am a Jewish man from Tarsus of Cilicia, a citizen of an important city. Now I ask you, let me speak to the people."

⁴⁰ After he had given permission, Paul stood on the steps and motioned with his hand to the people. When there was a great hush, he addressed them in Aramaic:

ACTS 22

¹ "Brothers and fathers, listen now to my defense before you." ² When they heard that he was addressing them in Aramaic, they became even quieter. ³ He continued, "I am a Jew, born in Tarsus of Cilicia but brought up in this city, educated at the feet of Gamaliel according to the strictness of our ancestral law. I was zealous for God, just as all of you are today. ⁴ I persecuted this Way to the death, arresting and putting both men and women in jail, ⁵ as both the high priest and the whole council of elders can testify about me. After I received letters from them to the brothers, I traveled to Damascus to arrest those who were there and bring them to Jerusalem to be punished.

PAUL'S TESTIMONY

⁶ "As I was traveling and approaching Damascus, about noon an intense light from heaven suddenly flashed around me. ⁷ I fell to the ground and heard a voice saying to me, 'Saul, Saul, why are you persecuting me?'

⁸ "I answered, 'Who are you, Lord?'

"He said to me, 'I am Jesus of Nazareth, the one you are persecuting.' ⁹ Now those who were with me saw the light, but they did not hear the voice of the one who was speaking to me.

¹⁰ "I said, 'What should I do, Lord?'

"The Lord told me, 'Get up and go into Damascus, and there you will be told everything that you have been assigned to do.'

11 "Since I couldn't see because of the brightness of the light, I was led by the hand by those who were with me, and went into Damascus. 12 Someone named Ananias, a devout man according to the law, who had a good reputation with all the Jews living there, 13 came and stood by me and said, 'Brother Saul, regain your sight.' And in that very hour I looked up and saw him. 14 And he said, 'The God of our ancestors has appointed you to know his will, to see the Righteous One, and to hear the words from his mouth, 15 since you will be a witness for him to all people of what you have seen and heard. 16 And now, why are you delaying? Get up and be baptized, and wash away your sins, calling on his name.'

17 "After I returned to Jerusalem and was praying in the temple, I fell into a trance 18 and saw him telling me, 'Hurry and get out of Jerusalem quickly, because they will not accept your testimony about me.'

19 "But I said, 'Lord, they know that in synagogue after synagogue I had those who believed in you imprisoned and beaten. 20 And when the blood of your witness Stephen was being shed, I stood there giving approval and guarding the clothes of those who killed him.'

21 "He said to me, 'Go, because I will send you far away to the Gentiles.'"

PAUL'S ROMAN PROTECTION

22 They listened to him up to this point. Then they raised their voices, shouting, "Wipe this man off the face of the earth! He should not be allowed to live!"

23 As they were yelling and flinging aside their garments and throwing dust into the air, 24 the commander ordered him to be brought into the barracks, directing that he be interrogated with the scourge to discover the reason they were shouting against him like this. 25 As they stretched him out for the lash, Paul said to the centurion standing by, "Is it legal for you to scourge a man who is a Roman citizen and is uncondemned?"

26 When the centurion heard this, he went and reported to the commander, saying, "What are you going to do? For this man is a Roman citizen."

27 The commander came and said to him, "Tell me, are you a Roman citizen?"

"Yes," he said.

28 The commander replied, "I bought this citizenship for a large amount of money."

"But I was born a citizen," Paul said.

29 So those who were about to examine him withdrew from him immediately. The commander too was alarmed when he realized Paul was a Roman citizen and he had bound him.

PAUL BEFORE THE SANHEDRIN

30 The next day, since he wanted to find out exactly why Paul was being accused by the Jews, he released him and instructed the chief priests and all the Sanhedrin to convene. He brought Paul down and placed him before them.

ACTS 23:1–11

1 Paul looked straight at the Sanhedrin and said, "Brothers, I have lived my life before God in all good conscience to this day."

2 The high priest Ananias ordered those who were standing next to him to strike him on the mouth. 3 Then Paul said to him, "God is going to strike you, you whitewashed wall! You are sitting there judging me according to the law, and yet in violation of the law are you ordering me to be struck?"

4 Those standing nearby said, "Do you dare revile God's high priest?"

5 "I did not know, brothers, that he was the high priest," replied Paul. "For it is written, You must not speak evil of a ruler of your people." 6 When Paul realized that one part of them were Sadducees and the other part were Pharisees, he cried out in the Sanhedrin, "Brothers, I am a Pharisee, a son of Pharisees. I am being judged because of the hope of the resurrection of the dead!" 7 When he said this, a dispute broke out between the Pharisees and the Sadducees, and the assembly was divided. 8 For the Sadducees say there is no

resurrection, and neither angel nor spirit, but the Pharisees affirm them all.

[9] The shouting grew loud, and some of the scribes of the Pharisees' party got up and argued vehemently, "We find nothing evil in this man. What if a spirit or an angel has spoken to him?"

[10] When the dispute became violent, the commander feared that Paul might be torn apart by them and ordered the troops to go down, take him away from them, and bring him into the barracks. [11] The following night, the Lord stood by him and said, "Have courage! For as you have testified about me in Jerusalem, so it is necessary for you to testify in Rome."

■ GOING DEEPER

HEBREWS 10:19-22

EXHORTATIONS TO GODLINESS

[19] Therefore, brothers and sisters, since we have boldness to enter the sanctuary through the blood of Jesus— [20] he has inaugurated for us a new and living way through the curtain (that is, through his flesh)— [21] and since we have a great high priest over the house of God, [22] let us draw near with a true heart in full assurance of faith, with our hearts sprinkled clean from an evil conscience and our bodies washed in pure water.

Notes

Week 5 Reflection

> Look over the key themes you marked in this week's readings. What did you notice about the Holy Spirit, the early Church, and the spread of the gospel?

> How do you see these themes at work in your life, community, and local church today?

One-Pot Chili

Try out this recipe at your next gathering! Prepare the meat and onions ahead of time, and ask each person to bring one or two of the remaining ingredients. As they arrive, add their ingredients to the pot and let your chili cook. By the time you finish discussing the reading from Acts, your chili should be ready to serve!

PREP TIME

20 minutes

COOK TIME

1 hour 15 minutes

SERVES

12–15

INGREDIENTS

1 tablespoon olive oil

1 medium red onion, finely diced

1 medium white onion, finely diced

1 pound ground beef

1 pound sausage (mild, regular, or spicy)

6 teaspoons chili powder

2 teaspoons sea salt

2 teaspoons black pepper

2 teaspoons granulated garlic

2 teaspoons paprika

2 teaspoons cumin

1 teaspoon cayenne pepper (optional)

3 (14.5-ounce) cans chili-ready diced tomatoes (one can with jalapeños)

1 (14.5-ounce) can Italian-style stewed tomatoes

1 (10-ounce) can Original Rotel®

2 (15.5-ounce) cans chili beans (regular or hot)

2 (15.5-ounce) cans black beans

1 (4-ounce) can diced green chilis

6 medium red potatoes, cut into small cubes with skin on

Optional Toppings:

Fried egg

Avocado, sliced

Sour cream

Shredded cheese

Hot sauce

INSTRUCTIONS

In a large pot, combine oil, onions, ground beef, and sausage over medium heat. Brown the meat, and remove any excess grease.

Combine all spices in a small bowl and set aside.

Add undrained cans of tomatoes, Rotel®, beans, and green chilis to pot. As you go, fill each empty can ¼ full with water and add to chili base.

Slowly stir in spices.

Add potatoes and reduce heat to low. Cover with a lid, leaving a small opening to vent. Let simmer for one hour, stirring occasionally, until potatoes are tender.

Add 1 to 2 cups water as needed until you reach your desired consistency.

Ladle into soup bowls, add desired toppings, and enjoy!

Grace Day

Take this day to catch up on your reading,
pray, and rest in the presence of the Lord.

HE WILL ALSO STRENGTHEN YOU TO THE

END, SO THAT YOU WILL BE BLAMELESS

IN THE DAY OF OUR LORD JESUS CHRIST.

1 Corinthians 1:8

Notes

Weekly Truth

Scripture is God breathed and true. When we memorize it, we carry the good news of Jesus with us wherever we go.

As we read Acts together, we are memorizing a portion of Peter's sermon in Acts 2. This week, memorize verse 39.

DATE

37 When they heard this, they were pierced to the heart and said to Peter and the rest of the apostles, "Brothers, what should we do?" 38 Peter replied, "Repent and be baptized, each of you, in the name of Jesus Christ for the forgiveness of your sins, and you will receive the gift of the Holy Spirit. 39 For the promise is for you and for your children, and for all who are far off, as many as the Lord our God will call."

Acts 2:37–39

SEE TIPS FOR MEMORIZING SCRIPTURE ON PAGE 196.

The Plot Against Paul

DAY 36

Acts 23:12–35; Psalm 40:16–17; 2 Corinthians 4:8–12

ACTS 23:12–35

THE PLOT AGAINST PAUL

¹² When it was morning, the Jews formed a conspiracy and bound themselves under a curse not to eat or drink until they had killed Paul. ¹³ There were more than forty who had formed this plot. ¹⁴ These men went to the chief priests and elders and said, "We have bound ourselves under a solemn curse that we won't eat anything until we have killed Paul. ¹⁵ So now you, along with the Sanhedrin, make a request to the commander that he bring him down to you as if you were going to investigate his case more thoroughly. But, before he gets near, we are ready to kill him."

¹⁶ But the son of Paul's sister, hearing about their ambush, came and entered the barracks and reported it to Paul. ¹⁷ Paul called one of the centurions and said, "Take this young man to the commander, because he has something to report to him."

¹⁸ So he took him, brought him to the commander, and said, "The prisoner Paul called me and asked me to bring this young man to you, because he has something to tell you."

¹⁹ The commander took him by the hand, led him aside, and inquired privately, "What is it you have to report to me?"

²⁰ "The Jews," he said, "have agreed to ask you to bring Paul down to the Sanhedrin tomorrow, as though they are going to hold a somewhat more careful inquiry about him.

²¹ Don't let them persuade you, because there are more than forty of them lying in ambush—

men who have bound themselves under a curse not to eat or drink until they have killed him. Now they are ready, waiting for your consent."

²² So the commander dismissed the young man and instructed him, "Don't tell anyone that you have informed me about this."

TO CAESAREA BY NIGHT

²³ He summoned two of his centurions and said, "Get two hundred soldiers ready with seventy cavalry and two hundred spearmen to go to Caesarea at nine tonight. ²⁴ Also provide mounts to ride so that Paul may be brought safely to Felix the governor."

²⁵ He wrote the following letter:

²⁶ Claudius Lysias,

To the most excellent governor Felix:

Greetings.

²⁷ When this man had been seized by the Jews and was about to be killed by them, I arrived with my troops and rescued him because I learned that he is a Roman citizen. ²⁸ Wanting to know the charge they were accusing him of, I brought him down before their Sanhedrin. ²⁹ I found out that the accusations were concerning questions of their law, and that there was no charge that merited death or imprisonment. ³⁰ When I was informed that there was a plot against the man, I sent him to you right away. I also ordered his accusers to state their case against him in your presence.

³¹ So the soldiers took Paul during the night and brought him to Antipatris as they were ordered. ³² The next day, they returned to the barracks, allowing the cavalry to go on with him. ³³ When these men entered Caesarea and delivered the letter to the governor, they also presented Paul to him. ³⁴ After he read it, he asked what province he was from. When he learned he was from Cilicia, ³⁵ he said, "I will give you a hearing whenever your accusers also get here." He ordered that he be kept under guard in Herod's palace.

◣ GOING DEEPER

PSALM 40:16-17

¹⁶ Let all who seek you rejoice and be glad in you;
let those who love your salvation continually say,
"The Lord is great!"
¹⁷ I am oppressed and needy;
may the Lord think of me.
You are my helper and my deliverer;
my God, do not delay.

2 CORINTHIANS 4:8-12

⁸ We are afflicted in every way but not crushed; we are perplexed but not in despair; ⁹ we are persecuted but not abandoned; we are struck down but not destroyed. ¹⁰ We always carry the death of Jesus in our body, so that the life of Jesus may also be displayed in our body. ¹¹ For we who live are always being given over to death for Jesus's sake, so that Jesus's life may also be displayed in our mortal flesh. ¹² So then, death is at work in us, but life in you.

Notes

DATE

I always strive to have
a clear conscience toward
God and men.

ACTS 24:16

Acts 24; Daniel 12:2–3; Philippians 1:12–19

Paul's Defense Before Felix

ACTS 24

THE ACCUSATION AGAINST PAUL

[1] Five days later Ananias the high priest came down with some elders and a lawyer named Tertullus. These men presented their case against Paul to the governor. [2] When Paul was called in, Tertullus began to accuse him and said, "We enjoy great peace because of you, and reforms are taking place for the benefit of this nation because of your foresight. [3] We acknowledge this in every way and everywhere, most excellent Felix, with utmost gratitude. [4] But, so that I will not burden you any further, I request that you would be kind enough to give us a brief hearing. [5] For we have found this man to be a plague, an agitator among all the Jews throughout the Roman world, and a ringleader of the sect of the Nazarenes. [6] He even tried to desecrate the temple, and so we apprehended him. [8] By examining him yourself you will be able to discern the truth about these charges we are bringing against him." [9] The Jews also joined in the attack, alleging that these things were true.

PAUL'S DEFENSE BEFORE FELIX

[10] When the governor motioned for him to speak, Paul replied, "Because I know you have been a judge of this nation for many years, I am glad to offer my defense in what concerns me. [11] You can verify for yourself that it is no more than twelve days since I went up to worship in Jerusalem. [12] They didn't find me arguing

with anyone or causing a disturbance among the crowd, either in the temple or in the synagogues or anywhere in the city. ¹³ Neither can they prove the charges they are now making against me. ¹⁴ But I admit this to you: I worship the God of my ancestors according to the Way, which they call a sect, believing everything that is in accordance with the law and written in the prophets. ¹⁵ I have a hope in God, which these men themselves also accept, that there will be a resurrection, both of the righteous and the unrighteous. ¹⁶ I always strive to have a clear conscience toward God and men. ¹⁷ After many years, I came to bring charitable gifts and offerings to my people. ¹⁸ While I was doing this, some Jews from Asia found me ritually purified in the temple, without a crowd and without any uproar. ¹⁹ It is they who ought to be here before you to bring charges, if they have anything against me. ²⁰ Or let these men here state what wrongdoing they found in me when I stood before the Sanhedrin, ²¹ other than this one statement I shouted while standing among them, 'Today I am on trial before you concerning the resurrection of the dead.'"

THE VERDICT POSTPONED

²² Since Felix was well informed about the Way, he adjourned the hearing, saying, "When Lysias the commander comes down, I will decide your case." ²³ He ordered that the centurion keep Paul under guard, though he could have some freedom, and that he should not prevent any of his friends from meeting his needs.

²⁴ Several days later, when Felix came with his wife Drusilla, who was Jewish, he sent for Paul and listened to him on the subject of faith in Christ Jesus. ²⁵ Now as he spoke about righteousness, self-control, and the judgment to come, Felix became afraid and replied, "Leave for now, but when I have an opportunity I'll call for you." ²⁶ At the same time he was also hoping that Paul would offer him money. So he sent for him quite often and conversed with him.

²⁷ After two years had passed, Porcius Festus succeeded Felix, and because Felix wanted to do the Jews a favor, he left Paul in prison.

♥ GOING DEEPER

DANIEL 12:2–3

² Many who sleep in the dust
of the earth will awake,
some to eternal life,
and some to disgrace and eternal contempt.
³ Those who have insight will shine
like the bright expanse of the heavens,
and those who lead many to righteousness,
like the stars forever and ever.

PHILIPPIANS 1:12–19

ADVANCE OF THE GOSPEL

¹² Now I want you to know, brothers and sisters, that what has happened to me has actually advanced the gospel, ¹³ so that it has become known throughout the whole imperial guard, and to everyone else, that my imprisonment is because I am in Christ. ¹⁴ Most of the brothers have gained confidence in the Lord from my imprisonment and dare even more to speak the word fearlessly. ¹⁵ To be sure, some preach Christ out of envy and rivalry, but others out of good will. ¹⁶ These preach out of love, knowing that I am appointed for the defense of the gospel; ¹⁷ the others proclaim Christ out of selfish ambition, not sincerely, thinking that they will cause me trouble in my imprisonment. ¹⁸ What does it matter? Only that in every way, whether from false motives or true, Christ is proclaimed, and in this I rejoice. Yes, and I will continue to rejoice ¹⁹ because I know this will lead to my salvation through your prayers and help from the Spirit of Jesus Christ.

Notes

DATE

Acts 25; 26; Job 33:4; Proverbs 2:6–8

Paul's Defense Before Agrippa

▶ **CAESAREA MARITIMA AD 59**

ACTS 25

APPEAL TO CAESAR

[1] Three days after Festus arrived in the province, he went up to Jerusalem from Caesarea. [2] The chief priests and the leaders of the Jews presented their case against Paul to him; and they appealed, [3] asking for a favor against Paul, that Festus summon him to Jerusalem. They were, in fact, preparing an ambush along the road to kill him. [4] Festus, however, answered that Paul should be kept at Caesarea, and that he himself was about to go there shortly. [5] "Therefore," he said, "let those of you who have authority go down with me and accuse him, if he has done anything wrong."

[6] When he had spent not more than eight or ten days among them, he went down to Caesarea. The next day, seated at the tribunal, he commanded Paul to be brought in. [7] When he arrived, the Jews who had come down from Jerusalem stood around him and brought many serious charges that they were not able to prove. [8] Then Paul made his defense: "Neither against the Jewish law, nor against the temple, nor against Caesar have I sinned in any way."

[9] But Festus, wanting to do the Jews a favor, replied to Paul, "Are you willing to go up to Jerusalem to be tried before me there on these charges?"

[10] Paul replied, "I am standing at Caesar's tribunal, where I ought to be tried. I have done no wrong to the Jews, as even you yourself know very well. [11] If then

I did anything wrong and am deserving of death, I am not trying to escape death; but if there is nothing to what these men accuse me of, no one can give me up to them. I appeal to Caesar!"

¹² Then after Festus conferred with his council, he replied, "You have appealed to Caesar; to Caesar you will go."

KING AGRIPPA AND BERNICE VISIT FESTUS

¹³ Several days later, King Agrippa and Bernice arrived in Caesarea and paid a courtesy call on Festus. ¹⁴ Since they were staying there several days, Festus presented Paul's case to the king, saying, "There's a man who was left as a prisoner by Felix. ¹⁵ When I was in Jerusalem, the chief priests and the elders of the Jews presented their case and asked that he be condemned. ¹⁶ I answered them that it is not the Roman custom to give someone up before the accused faces the accusers and has an opportunity for a defense against the charges. ¹⁷ So when they had assembled here, I did not delay. The next day I took my seat at the tribunal and ordered the man to be brought in. ¹⁸ The accusers stood up but brought no charge against him of the evils I was expecting. ¹⁹ Instead they had some disagreements with him about their own religion and about a certain Jesus, a dead man Paul claimed to be alive. ²⁰ Since I was at a loss in a dispute over such things, I asked him if he wanted to go to Jerusalem and be tried there regarding these matters. ²¹ But when Paul appealed to be held for trial by the Emperor, I ordered him to be kept in custody until I could send him to Caesar."

²² Agrippa said to Festus, "I would like to hear the man myself."

"Tomorrow you will hear him," he replied.

PAUL BEFORE AGRIPPA

²³ So the next day, Agrippa and Bernice came with great pomp and entered the auditorium with the military commanders and prominent men of the city. When Festus gave the command, Paul was brought in. ²⁴ Then Festus said, "King Agrippa and all men present with us, you see this man. The whole Jewish community has appealed to me concerning him, both in Jerusalem and here, shouting that he should not live any longer. ²⁵ I found that he had not done anything deserving of death, but when he himself appealed to the

Emperor, I decided to send him. ²⁶ I have nothing definite to write to my lord about him. Therefore, I have brought him before all of you, and especially before you, King Agrippa, so that after this examination is over, I may have something to write. ²⁷ For it seems unreasonable to me to send a prisoner without indicating the charges against him."

ACTS 26

PAUL'S DEFENSE BEFORE AGRIPPA

¹ Agrippa said to Paul, "You have permission to speak for yourself."

Then Paul stretched out his hand and began his defense: ² "I consider myself fortunate that it is before you, King Agrippa, I am to make my defense today against all the accusations of the Jews, ³ especially since you are very knowledgeable about all the Jewish customs and controversies. Therefore I beg you to listen to me patiently.

⁴ "All the Jews know my way of life from my youth, which was spent from the beginning among my own people and in Jerusalem. ⁵ They have known me for a long time, if they are willing to testify, that according to the strictest sect of our religion I lived as a Pharisee. ⁶ And now I stand on trial because of the hope in what God promised to our ancestors, ⁷ the promise our twelve tribes hope to reach as they earnestly serve him night and day. King Agrippa, I am being accused by the Jews because of this hope. ⁸ Why do any of you consider it incredible that God raises the dead? ⁹ In fact, I myself was convinced that it was necessary to do many things in opposition to the name of Jesus of Nazareth. ¹⁰ I actually did this in Jerusalem, and I locked up many of the saints in prison, since I had received authority for that from the chief priests. When they were put to death, I was in agreement against them. ¹¹ In all the synagogues I often punished them and tried to make them blaspheme. Since I was terribly enraged at them, I pursued them even to foreign cities.

PAUL'S ACCOUNT OF HIS CONVERSION AND COMMISSION

¹² "I was traveling to Damascus under these circumstances with authority and a commission from the chief priests. ¹³ King Agrippa, while on the road at midday, I saw a light from heaven brighter than the sun, shining around me and

those traveling with me. ¹⁴ We all fell to the ground, and I heard a voice speaking to me in Aramaic, 'Saul, Saul, why are you persecuting me? It is hard for you to kick against the goads.'

¹⁵ "I asked, 'Who are you, Lord?'

"And the Lord replied, 'I am Jesus, the one you are persecuting. ¹⁶ But get up and stand on your feet. For I have appeared to you for this purpose, to appoint you as a servant and a witness of what you have seen and will see of me. ¹⁷ I will rescue you from your people and from the Gentiles. I am sending you to them ¹⁸ to open their eyes so that they may turn from darkness to light and from the power of Satan to God, that they may receive forgiveness of sins and a share among those who are sanctified by faith in me.'

¹⁹ "So then, King Agrippa, I was not disobedient to the heavenly vision. ²⁰ Instead, I preached to those in Damascus first, and to those in Jerusalem and in all the region of Judea, and to the Gentiles, that they should repent and turn to God, and do works worthy of repentance. ²¹ For this reason the Jews seized me in the temple and were trying to kill me. ²² To this very day, I have had help from God, and I stand and testify to both small and great, saying nothing other than what the prophets and Moses said would take place— ²³ that the Messiah would suffer, and that, as the first to rise from the dead, he would proclaim light to our people and to the Gentiles."

AGRIPPA NOT QUITE PERSUADED

²⁴ As he was saying these things in his defense, Festus exclaimed in a loud voice, "You're out of your mind, Paul! Too much study is driving you mad."

²⁵ But Paul replied, "I'm not out of my mind, most excellent Festus. On the contrary, I'm speaking words of truth and good judgment. ²⁶ For the king knows about these matters, and I can speak boldly to him. For I am convinced that none of these things has escaped his notice, since this was not done in a corner. ²⁷ King Agrippa, do you believe the prophets? I know you believe."

²⁸ Agrippa said to Paul, "Are you going to persuade me to become a Christian so easily?"

²⁹ "I wish before God," replied Paul, "that whether easily or with difficulty, not only you but all who listen to me today might become as I am—except for these chains."

³⁰ The king, the governor, Bernice, and those sitting with them got up, ³¹ and when they had left they talked with each other and said, "This man is not doing anything to deserve death or imprisonment."

³² Agrippa said to Festus, "This man could have been released if he had not appealed to Caesar."

◗ GOING DEEPER

JOB 33:4

The Spirit of God has made me,
and the breath of the Almighty gives me life.

PROVERBS 2:6-8

⁶ For the LORD gives wisdom;
from his mouth come knowledge and understanding.
⁷ He stores up success for the upright;
He is a shield for those who live with integrity

⁸ so that he may guard the paths of justice
and protect the way of his faithful followers.

Notes

DATE

IT IS THE HOPE OF CHRIST THAT MAKES IT POSSIBLE FOR

US TO PERSEVERE IN TIMES OF TRIBULATION AND DISTRESS.

WE HAVE AN ANCHOR FOR OUR SOULS THAT RESTS IN THE

ONE WHO HAS GONE BEFORE US AND CONQUERED.

R. C. Sproul

Acts 27; 28:1–10; Psalm 37:28; Mark 16:17–18

The Storm-Tossed Ship

**CAESAREA MARITIMA
AND MALTA
AD 59**

ACTS 27

SAILING FOR ROME

[1] When it was decided that we were to sail to Italy, they handed over Paul and some other prisoners to a centurion named Julius, of the Imperial Regiment. [2] When we had boarded a ship of Adramyttium, we put to sea, intending to sail to ports along the coast of Asia. Aristarchus, a Macedonian of Thessalonica, was with us. [3] The next day we put in at Sidon, and Julius treated Paul kindly and allowed him to go to his friends to receive their care. [4] When we had put out to sea from there, we sailed along the northern coast of Cyprus because the winds were against us. [5] After sailing through the open sea off Cilicia and Pamphylia, we reached Myra in Lycia. [6] There the centurion found an Alexandrian ship sailing for Italy and put us on board. [7] Sailing slowly for many days, with difficulty we arrived off Cnidus. Since the wind did not allow us to approach it, we sailed along the south side of Crete off Salmone. [8] With still more difficulty we sailed along the coast and came to a place called Fair Havens near the city of Lasea.

PAUL'S ADVICE IGNORED

[9] By now much time had passed, and the voyage was already dangerous. Since the Day of Atonement was already over, Paul gave his advice [10] and told them, "Men, I can see that this voyage is headed toward disaster and heavy loss, not only of the cargo and the ship but also of our lives." [11] But the centurion paid attention to the captain and the owner of the ship rather than to what Paul said. [12] Since

the harbor was unsuitable to winter in, the majority decided to set sail from there, hoping somehow to reach Phoenix, a harbor on Crete facing the southwest and northwest, and to winter there.

STORM-TOSSED SHIP

[13] When a gentle south wind sprang up, they thought they had achieved their purpose. They weighed anchor and sailed along the shore of Crete. [14] But before long, a fierce wind called the "northeaster" rushed down from the island. [15] Since the ship was caught and unable to head into the wind, we gave way to it and were driven along. [16] After running under the shelter of a little island called Cauda, we were barely able to get control of the skiff. [17] After hoisting it up, they used ropes and tackle and girded the ship. Fearing they would run aground on the Syrtis, they lowered the drift-anchor, and in this way they were driven along. [18] Because we were being severely battered by the storm, they began to jettison the cargo the next day. [19] On the third day, they threw the ship's tackle overboard with their own hands. [20] For many days neither sun nor stars appeared, and the severe storm kept raging. Finally all hope was fading that we would be saved.

[21] Since they had been without food for a long time, Paul then stood up among them and said, "You men should have followed my advice not to sail from Crete and sustain this damage and loss.

[22] Now I urge you to take courage,

because there will be no loss of any of your lives, but only of the ship. [23] For last night an angel of the God I belong to and serve stood by me [24] and said, 'Don't be afraid, Paul. It is necessary for you to appear before Caesar. And indeed, God has graciously given you all those who are sailing with you.' [25] So take courage, men, because I believe God that it will be just the way it was told to me. [26] But we have to run aground on some island."

[27] When the fourteenth night came, we were drifting in the Adriatic Sea, and about midnight the sailors thought they were approaching land. [28] They took soundings and found it to be a hundred twenty feet deep; when they had sailed a little farther and sounded again, they found it to be ninety feet deep. [29] Then, fearing we might run aground on the rocks, they dropped four anchors from the stern and prayed for daylight to come. [30] Some sailors tried to escape from the ship; they had let down the skiff into the sea, pretending that they were going to put out anchors from the bow. [31] Paul said to the centurion and the soldiers, "Unless these men stay in the ship, you cannot be saved." [32] Then the soldiers cut the ropes holding the skiff and let it drop away.

[33] When it was about daylight, Paul urged them all to take food, saying, "Today is the fourteenth day that you have been waiting and going without food, having eaten nothing. [34] So I urge you to take some food. For this is for your survival, since none of you will lose a hair from your head." [35] After he said these things and had taken some bread, he gave thanks to God in the presence of all of them, and after he broke it, he began to eat. [36] They all were encouraged and took food themselves. [37] In all there were 276 of us on the ship. [38] When they had eaten enough, they began to lighten the ship by throwing the grain overboard into the sea.

SHIPWRECK

[39] When daylight came, they did not recognize the land but sighted a bay with a beach. They planned to run the ship ashore if they could. [40] After cutting loose the anchors, they left them in the sea, at the same time loosening the ropes that held the rudders. Then they hoisted the foresail to the wind and headed for the beach. [41] But they struck a sandbar and ran the ship aground. The bow jammed fast and remained immovable, while the stern began to break up by the pounding of the waves. [42] The soldiers' plan was to kill the prisoners so that no one could swim away and escape. [43] But the centurion kept them from carrying out their plan because he wanted to save Paul, and so he ordered those who could swim to jump overboard first and get to land. [44] The rest were to follow, some on planks and some on debris from the ship. In this way, everyone safely reached the shore.

ACTS 28:1–10

MALTA'S HOSPITALITY

[1] Once safely ashore, we then learned that the island was called Malta. [2] The local people showed us extraordinary

kindness. They lit a fire and took us all in, since it was raining and cold. ³ As Paul gathered a bundle of brushwood and put it on the fire, a viper came out because of the heat and fastened itself on his hand. ⁴ When the local people saw the snake hanging from his hand, they said to one another, "This man, no doubt, is a murderer. Even though he has escaped the sea, Justice has not allowed him to live." ⁵ But he shook the snake off into the fire and suffered no harm. ⁶ They expected that he would begin to swell up or suddenly drop dead. After they waited a long time and saw nothing unusual happen to him, they changed their minds and said he was a god.

MINISTRY IN MALTA

⁷ Now in the area around that place was an estate belonging to the leading man of the island, named Publius, who welcomed us and entertained us hospitably for three days. ⁸ Publius's father was in bed suffering from fever and dysentery. Paul went to him, and praying and laying his hands on him, he healed him. ⁹ After this, the rest of those on the island who had diseases also came and were healed. ¹⁰ So they heaped many honors on us, and when we sailed, they gave us what we needed.

❦ GOING DEEPER

PSALM 37:28

For the LORD loves justice
and will not abandon his faithful ones.
They are kept safe forever,
but the children of the wicked will be destroyed.

MARK 16:17-18

¹⁷ "And these signs will accompany those who believe: In my name they will drive out demons; they will speak in new tongues; ¹⁸ they will pick up snakes; if they should drink anything deadly, it will not harm them; they will lay hands on the sick, and they will get well."

Notes

DATE

Acts 28:11–31; Isaiah 6:9–10; 2 Timothy 4:6–8

Rome at Last

ROME
AD 59–62

ACTS 28:11–31

ROME AT LAST

[11] After three months we set sail in an Alexandrian ship that had wintered at the island, with the Twin Gods as its figurehead. [12] Putting in at Syracuse, we stayed three days. [13] From there, after making a circuit along the coast, we reached Rhegium. After one day a south wind sprang up, and the second day we came to Puteoli. [14] There we found brothers and sisters and were invited to stay a week with them. And so we came to Rome. [15] Now the brothers and sisters from there had heard the news about us and had come to meet us as far as the Forum of Appius and the Three Taverns. When Paul saw them, he thanked God and took courage. [16] When we entered Rome, Paul was allowed to live by himself with the soldier who guarded him.

PAUL'S FIRST INTERVIEW WITH ROMAN JEWS

[17] After three days he called together the leaders of the Jews. When they had gathered he said to them, "Brothers, although I have done nothing against our people or the customs of our ancestors, I was delivered as a prisoner from Jerusalem into the hands of the Romans. [18] After they examined me, they wanted to release me, since there was no reason for the death penalty in my case. [19] Because the Jews objected, I was compelled to appeal to Caesar; even though I had no charge to bring against my people. [20] For this reason I've asked to see you and speak to you. In fact, it is for the hope of Israel that I'm wearing this chain."

WEEK 6

²¹ Then they said to him, "We haven't received any letters about you from Judea. None of the brothers has come and reported or spoken anything evil about you. ²² But we want to hear what your views are, since we know that people everywhere are speaking against this sect."

THE RESPONSE TO PAUL'S MESSAGE

²³ After arranging a day with him, many came to him at his lodging. From dawn to dusk he expounded and testified about the kingdom of God. He tried to persuade them about Jesus from both the Law of Moses and the Prophets. ²⁴ Some were persuaded by what he said, but others did not believe.

²⁵ Disagreeing among themselves, they began to leave after Paul made one statement: "The Holy Spirit was right in saying to your ancestors through the prophet Isaiah ²⁶ when he said,

> Go to these people and say:
> You will always be listening,
> but never understanding;
> and you will always be looking,
> but never perceiving.
> ²⁷ For the hearts of these people
> have grown callous,
> their ears are hard of hearing,
> and they have shut their eyes;
> otherwise they might see with their eyes
> and hear with their ears,
> understand with their heart
> and turn,
> and I would heal them.

²⁸ Therefore, let it be known to you that this salvation of God has been sent to the Gentiles; they will listen."

PAUL'S MINISTRY UNHINDERED

³⁰ Paul stayed two whole years in his own rented house. And he welcomed all who visited him, ³¹ proclaiming the kingdom of God and teaching about the Lord Jesus Christ with all boldness and without hindrance.

⚓ GOING DEEPER

ISAIAH 6:9–10

⁹ And he replied:

> Go! Say to these people:
> Keep listening, but do not understand;
> keep looking, but do not perceive.
> ¹⁰ Make the minds of these people dull;
> deafen their ears and blind their eyes;
> otherwise they might see with their eyes
> and hear with their ears,
> understand with their minds,
> turn back, and be healed.

2 TIMOTHY 4:6–8

⁶ For I am already being poured out as a drink offering, and the time for my departure is close. ⁷ I have fought the good fight, I have finished the race, I have kept the faith. ⁸ There is reserved for me the crown of righteousness, which the Lord, the righteous Judge, will give me on that day, and not only to me, but to all those who have loved his appearing.

Notes

DATE

Week 6 Reflection

▶ Look over the key themes you marked in this week's readings. What did you notice about the Holy Spirit, the early Church, and the spread of the gospel?

▶ How do you see these themes at work in your life,
community, and local church today?

Grace Day

Take this day to catch up on your reading,
pray, and rest in the presence of the Lord.

THE SPIRIT OF GOD HAS MADE ME, AND THE

BREATH OF THE ALMIGHTY GIVES ME LIFE.

Job 33:4

Notes

Weekly Truth

Scripture is God breathed and true. When we memorize it, we carry the good news of Jesus with us wherever we go.

As we've read Acts together, we've been memorizing a portion of Peter's sermon in Acts 2. Test your memory by filling in the blanks on the following page.

DATE

37 When they heard this, they were _____ to the heart and ____ to _____ and the rest of the _____, "Brothers, what _____ ___ ___?" 38 Peter replied, "_____ and be _____, each of you, in the name of _____ _____ for the _____ of your sins, and you will receive the ___ of the Holy Spirit. 39 For the _____ is for you and for your _____, and for all who are ___ ___, as many as the Lord our God will ___."

Acts 2:37–39

SEE TIPS FOR MEMORIZING SCRIPTURE ON PAGE 196.

BENEDICTION

▼

SO, THEN, YOU ARE NO LONGER FOREIGNERS AND STRANGERS, BUT FELLOW

CITIZENS WITH THE SAINTS, AND MEMBERS OF GOD'S HOUSEHOLD, BUILT

ON THE FOUNDATION OF THE APOSTLES AND PROPHETS, WITH CHRIST

JESUS HIMSELF AS THE CORNERSTONE.

Ephesians 2:19–20

Tips for Memorizing Scripture

At She Reads Truth, we believe Scripture memorization is an important discipline in your walk with God. Committing God's Word to memory means we carry it with us and we can minister to others wherever we go. As you approach the Weekly Truth passage in this book, try these memorization tips to see which techniques work best for you!

STUDY IT

Study the passage in its biblical context, and ask yourself a few questions before you begin to memorize it: What does this passage say? What does it mean? How would I say this in my own words? What does it teach me about God? Understanding what the passage means helps you know why it is important to carry it with you wherever you go.

Break the passage into smaller sections, memorizing a phrase at a time.

PRAY IT

Use the passage you are memorizing as a prompt for prayer.

WRITE IT

Dedicate a notebook to Scripture memorization, and write the passage over and over again.

Diagram the passage after you write it out. Place a square around the verbs, underline the nouns, and circle any adjectives or adverbs. Say the passage aloud several times, emphasizing the verbs as you repeat it. Then do the same thing again with the nouns, then the adjectives and adverbs.

Write out the first letter of each word in the passage somewhere you can reference it throughout the week as you work on your memorization.

Use a whiteboard to write out the passage. Erase a few words at a time as you continue to repeat it aloud. Keep erasing parts of the passage until you have it all committed to memory.

CREATE

If you can, make up a tune for the passage to sing as you go about your day, or try singing it to the tune of a favorite song.

Sketch the passage, visualizing what each phrase would look like in the form of a picture. Or try using calligraphy or altering the style of your handwriting as you write it out.

Use hand signals or signs to come up with associations for each word or phrase, and repeat the movements as you practice.

SAY IT

Repeat the passage out loud to yourself as you are going through the rhythm of your day—getting ready, pouring your coffee, waiting in traffic, or making dinner.

Listen to the passage read aloud to you.

Record a voice memo on your phone, and listen to it throughout the day, or play it on an audio Bible.

SHARE IT

Memorize the passage with a friend, family member, or mentor. Spontaneously challenge each other to recite the passage, or pick a time to review your passage and practice saying it from memory together.

Send the passage as an encouraging text to a friend, testing yourself as you type to see how much you have memorized so far.

KEEP AT IT!

Set reminders on your phone to prompt you to practice your passage.

Purchase a She Reads Truth Scripture Card Set, or keep a stack of note cards with Scripture you are memorizing by your bed. Practice reciting what you've memorized previously before you go to sleep, ending with the passages you are currently learning. If you wake up in the middle of the night, review them again instead of grabbing your phone. Read them out loud before you get out of bed in the morning.

CSB BOOK ABBREVIATIONS

BIBLIOGRAPHY

The Book of Common Prayer and Administration of the Sacraments and Other Rites and Ceremonies of the Church. The Church Hymnal Corporation and The Seabury Press, 1789. Reprint, Kingsport Press, 1977.

Nässelqvist, Dan. "Apostle." In *The Lexham Bible Dictionary,* edited by John D. Barry, David Bomar, and Derek R. Brown, et al. Lexham Press, 2016.

Polhill, John B. *Acts.* Vol. 26. The New American Commentary. Broadman & Holman Publishers, 1992.

Sproul, R. C. *Surprised by Suffering.* Tyndale House Publishers, Inc., 1998.

Wright, N. T. *Surprised by Hope: Rethinking Heaven, the Resurrection, and the Mission of the Church.* HarperCollins, 2008.

You just spent 42 days in the Word of God!

MY FAVORITE DAY OF
THIS READING PLAN:

ONE THING I LEARNED
ABOUT GOD:

WHAT WAS GOD DOING IN
MY LIFE DURING THIS STUDY?

HOW DID I FIND DELIGHT IN GOD'S WORD?

WHAT DID I LEARN THAT I WANT TO SHARE
WITH SOMEONE ELSE?

A SPECIFIC PASSAGE OR VERSE
THAT ENCOURAGED ME:

A SPECIFIC PASSAGE OR VERSE THAT
CHALLENGED AND CONVICTED ME: